DISCARD

CRICUT FOR BEGINNERS

The Ultimate Beginners Guide to Become a Master of the Cricut Machine. Practical and Detailed Step-by-Step Guide to Craft and Design, with Creative Project Ideas and Examples.

AUTHOR

Sarah Explore

© **Copyright 2019 by Sarah Explore.**
  All Rights Reserved.

This document is geared towards providing exact and reliable information in regards to the topic and issue covered. The publication is sold with the idea that the publisher is not required to render accounting, officially permitted, or otherwise, qualified services. If advice is necessary, legal or professional, a practiced individual in the profession should be ordered.

From a Declaration of Principles which was accepted and approved by a Committee of the American Bar Association and a Committee of Publishers and Associations.

In no way is it legal to reproduce, duplicate, or transmit any part of this document in either electronic means or in printed format. Recording of this publication is strictly prohibited and any storage of this document is not allowed unless with written permission from the publisher. All rights reserved.

The information provided herein is stated to be truthful and consistent, in that any liability, in terms of inattention or otherwise, by any usage or abuse of any policies, processes, or directions contained within is the solitary and utter responsibility of the recipient reader. Under no circumstances will any legal responsibility or blame be held against the publisher for any reparation, damages, or monetary loss due to the information herein, either directly or indirectly.

Respective authors own all copyrights not held by the publisher.

The information herein is offered for informational purposes solely, and is universal as so. The presentation of the information is without contract or any type of guarantee assurance.

The trademarks that are used are without any consent, and the publication of the trademark is without permission or backing by the trademark owner. All trademarks and brands within this book are for clarifying purposes only and are owned by the owners themselves, not affiliated with this document.

Table of content

Chapter One: Introduction 8

Chapter Two: How To Use Cricut Machine (Cricut Expression 2)...63

Chapter Three: Setting a New Cricut Machine Up Using Software(Load And Unload Paper)...122

Chapter Three: Maintenance Of The Cricut Machine...128

Chapter Four: What materials would I be able to cut with my Cricut?...................................156

Chapter One

Introduction

What is a Cricut Machine?

A Cricut is a cutting machine – that is the short answer – that enables you to cut and make wonderful and glorious artworks with materials you didn't know existed. Contingent upon the model you have you can likewise draw, decorate and make collapsing lines to make 3D ventures, welcoming cards, boxes, and so on.

The Cricut is an extraordinary machine for individuals that adore creating, and for or individuals that need to cut a lot of things and various sorts of materials.

Or

While the brand incorporates a few distinct items, including heat presses and embossers, the word Cricut has gotten synonymous with die-cutting machines. So in case, you're wondering, what is a Cricut machine? The appropriate response is a home die-cutting machine utilized for paper creating and different expressions and specialties.

Basically, it's a keen cutting machine known as the "immaculate passage point to the universe of accurate crafting."

It's critical to realize that these machines are not just utilized for cutting paper. They're made to cut a wide assortment of material in stunning manners. Vinyl is another material that is related to kick the bucket cutting machines, just as felt, card stock thus numerous others. They can even cut wood!

Notwithstanding cutting a wide range of materials, the machines that are currently accessible can likewise draw with pens, compose with pens and score material for fresh, simple collapsing.

Note: If you're here pondering, what is a cricket cutting machine? or then again Where to purchase a cricket shaper? You're additionally in the ideal spot! Cricut is a brand name that is articulated "cricket."

In case you're hearing "cricket" in connection to cutting, paper, vinyl or pretty much anything sly, all things considered, you're truly tuning in to somebody talk about Cricut.

What does a Cricut machine accompany?

There are a few distinct models, and the things that accompany each machine shift among them. Yet, there are a few things that all around accompany all machines.

Each Cricut accompanies:
- A Cricut cutting machine

- A top-notch fine-point blade and sharp edge lodging
- A 12×12" LightGrip cutting mat
- A USB link
- A force connector
- An invite direct for a simple arrangement
- Free preliminary enrollment to Cricut Access
- Access to 25 free, prepared to-make ventures
- Materials for a training venture.

A few models accompany more things, as various sharp blades, scoring wheels or an exceptional pen for composing.

What does a CricutMachine do?

Since you realize that this machine is a bite the dust shaper, I'm certain you're thinking about what makes it so exceptional. What does a Cricut do to paper and different materials that make it worth far beyond a couple of scissors?

Making the card utilized the entirety of the cutting machine's basic capacities. To start with, It cut out the card shape, slice cuts to embed a little bit of card stock and cut that bit of card stock. At that point, it drew swirly lines with a pen and composed a welcome with that equivalent pen. At last, it scored the card for folding.

How does a Cricut work?

Your PC, tablet or cell phone associated with your machine to send your picked plan (otherwise called a cut document) to the cutting machine. The plan demonstrates if each line ought to be cut, composed with a pen or scored. The machine wraps up!

How would you make Cricut designs?

Each machine utilizes its very own image programming, and it's allowed to download and utilize. You can even utilize the Cricut Design Space application!

Configuration Space is very easy to understand. You can make designs without any preparation and transfer pictures. You can likewise import cut documents made by others, buy plans legitimately inside the application and change any of those structures to tweak them.

Is Cricut Design Space hard to utilize?

No. It's in this way, thus, so natural to utilize! I've utilized a wide range of configuration programs consistently, and I've certainly battled with some of them.

The Cricut Design Space programming is as straightforward as it can be while as yet giving you the opportunity to be innovative with your plans and activities.

How does Cricut Design Space Work?

DesignSpace resembles your formula for your project. What you make in Design Space just advises your machine where to cut, score or compose.

When your machine is associated with your PC or another gadget, the cutting machine can simply finish a full structure if there's just one stage.

If there are numerous means, your Cricut will convey guidelines to show on your PC or gadget screen. It can let you know whether and when you have to do other undertaking steps. For instance, it will guide you to stack your next piece of paper (or other material) or swap various shades of pens.

What are the Types of Cricut Machines Available?

There are two arrangements of Cricut cutting machines as of now available: the Explore arrangement and the Cricut Maker.

The Explore Series incorporates:

- Cricut Explore One
- Cricut Explore Air
- Cricut Explore Air 2

The distinctive Explorer models come in different colors, with the Cricut Explore Air 2 being accessible in at least 12 colors over a few retailers.

The Maker is a solitary model that as of now comes in three distinct hues: champagne, blue and pink.

What's the contrast between a Cricut Explore and a Cricut Maker?

The Explore One is the most fundamental cutting machine in the brand's lineup, which makes it the least expensive, while the Cricut Explore Air 2 is the freshest Explore model.

It likewise has the most highlights. It has the most significant expense of the three Explore cutting machines. The Maker is presently in classification without anyone else's input, with a bigger number of highlights and capacities than some other machine. There is one model and it comes in three distinct hues.

The Cricut Maker is the most adaptable brilliant cutting machine in the lineup, and it's known as "a definitive savvy cutting machine."

It bridles every one of the elements of the Cricut Explore Air 2 with extra highlights like a scoring haggles sharp edge making up toolset that can compose, cut and score more materials than any time in recent memory.

The Maker is additionally the just one in the lineup with the versatile device framework. It's a cutting innovation that controls the bearing of the edge and the weight with a moving activity. This enables it to best work with the material.

What would you be able to do with a Cricut? Or on the other hand what can a Cricut make?

Since you know what a Cricut machine is and the nuts and bolts of what it does, you may in any case be pondering, what makes it so incredible?

I realize I didn't get it when the idea of a kick the bucket cutting machine was first disclosed it to me. It required some investment for me to see precisely what it was prepared to do.

I know a ton of you are here in light of the fact that you're pondering, what can a Cricut do? Or then again what would you be able to make with a Cricut?

The appropriate response is; you can make such a lot of stuff!

Anyway, what would you be able to do with a Cricut?

Coming up next is a rundown of the most mainstream things it can make:

- Plan and cut out letters, words and shapes for scrapbooking.
- Structure and cut out your instructor gratefulness blessings.
- Work out words and statements for scrapbooking and marks.
- Address envelopes with perfect textual styles.
- Structure and cut out stickers for your organizer, schedule or whatever else.
- Make high quality, custom cards for birthday celebrations, commemorations, extraordinary events and that's just the beginning.
- Plan and make custom child onesies.
- Plan and cut out hand crafted cake toppers for wonderful dribble cakes.
- Plan and make custom shirts and sweatshirts.
- Plan or cut out stencils for inside canvas.
- Make divider decals.

- Cut out special stickers for your Erin Condren organizer.
- Make confined statement fine art.
- Make monogram or organizing cushions.
- Make a calfskin armlet.
- Make custom hoops.
- Plan or make your own Christmas trimmings.
- Make occasion or gathering adornments.
- Make a canine tag for your hide infant.
- Make enrichments for custom made wine glasses, mugs and tumblers.
- Make decals for anything you need to tweak.
- Design standard plates to make them one of a kind.
- Make wash room, storeroom or authoritative marks.
- Make and cut out window decals.
- Cut out buntings and pennants.
- Modify socks into amusing blessings.
- Make and cut out custom vinyl vehicle stickers.
- Cut out structures for diy glass drawing.
- Make a painted or provincial wooden sign.
- Cut out appliqués or blanket squares.

... and innumerable other DIY or sly tasks. There are truly beyond any reasonable amount to incorporate here!

Is a Cricut cutting machine a printer?

Does a Cricut print? Numerous individuals believe that it's a printer, and I can perceive any reason why! At the point when a machine can accomplish such a great deal, it's anything but difficult to expect it can do for all intents and purposes anything shrewd!

It could be said, a Cricut is a printer, however not the manner in which you think. You can utilize different pens in your machine to print, compose or draw what you make, make and structure.

For instance, you can address envelopes in excellent, scripty textual styles. You can compose letters from Santa with a bona-fide looking penmanship text style. You can compose welcome in your handcrafted cards or sign your name in a mark. You can even monogram your undertakings with an exclusively, spared monogram or image to recognize your work!

I wasn't joking when I said there were an assortment of pens!

Truly, you'll discover any shading you need, with various completions (shiny, metallic, and marker-like) and widths. You'll likewise discover pens for various purposes. Specifically, there are launderable texture pens to stamp your material, calligraphy pens for impeccable content and numerous different styles.

That being stated, a Cricut isn't a printer. Be that as it may, notwithstanding the pens and composing capacities, it approaches with its Print at that point Cut usefulness.

Print Then Cut enables you to get any plan any shading to your undertakings. You can make structures that distinguish the zones that ought to be imprinted on vinyl, heat-move vinyl, paper or different materials. After the structure has been printed, you at that point transmit it right to your machine for cutting it where you need it cut.

Confounded? I thoroughly comprehend! There are such a large number of approaches to utilize the Print Then Cut component, and I confess to being totally lost with respect to how and when it could be utilized when I previously caught wind of it.

One supportive approach to comprehend Print Then Cut it is to consider making your own stickers.

For instance, Check out these DIY organizer stickers in the above picture. In the first place, the different hues and work of art were printed out in shading on sticker paper. At that point the stickers were removed in absolutely the correct structure with the machine.

What can a Cricut cut?

If, subsequent to perusing the above area about what would you be able to do with a Cricut, you're still under the feeling that it can just cut paper for scrapbooking reasons for existing, you're off-base.

Initially, you missed a great deal. You have to look up and read that area once more.

Second, get ready to have your mind blown, in light of the fact that the data I'm going to share will astound you!

I've assembled a rundown of everything any of these presently accessible cutting machines can cut. In case you're pondering about the particular material that a Maker can cut, you'll need to look down, however not very quick! The Cricut Maker can cut everything any of the Explore machines can cut, in addition to additional.

To put it plainly, you'll have to read the two areas.

What can a Cricut Explore Air 2, Explore Air and an Explore One cut?

- Paper
- Vinyl
- Cement vinyl (additionally now and then called paper vinyl)
- Iron-on move vinyl
- Card stock

Notice board

Texture, including oil material, silk, polyester, denim and felt (in the wake of settling with HeatnBond)

- Art froth
- Plug board
- Wax paper
- Aluminum foil
- Washi paper and Washi tape

- Wrapping paper
- Development paper
- Material paper
- Sheet channel tape
- Window stick vinyl
- Artificial softened cowhide
- Sticker paper
- Paper basic food item sacks
- Cowhide up to 2.0mm thick
- Artificial calfskin up to 1.0mm thick
- Printable texture
- attractive sheets
- aint chips
- Vellum
- Canvas
- Photograph paper
- Wood, birch, up to 0.5mm thick
- Chipboard up to 2.0mm thick
- Fake calfskin
- Cardboard
- Folded cardboard
- Aluminum metal up to 0.14mm thick
- Fleece felt
- Stencil film
- Straightforwardness film

- Tattoo paper

What can a Cricut Maker Cut?

A Cricut Maker can cut everything a Cricut Explore Air 2, an Explore Air and an Explore Air 2 can cut. It can likewise cut essentially any sort of texture.

You may have seen that there are a few kinds of texture on the rundown of what the Explore arrangement can cut, yet all must be settled with HeatnBond.

HeatnBond is a texture backing that you iron onto the texture. It's regularly used to connect one texture to another, however when you use it before cutting it prevents the texture from fraying or destroying.

The greatest distinction between what a Cricut Maker can cut and what a Cricut Explore machine can cut is texture.

To start with, you don't have to balance out the texture before having the Maker cut it. That implies you can utilize pretty much any texture directly from the texture store without any planning or extra materials. (Keep in mind, the Explore arrangement expects you to treat your textures with HeatnBond before cutting.)

Second, the Maker has a rotating sharp edge, which is distinctive strategy for cutting than every single other machine that preceded it.

The turning edge isn't only a sharp edge on a wheel. It's an edge that twists and bends with a floating and moving movement. That moving activity enables your Cricut to slice from side-to-side, here and there and any heading in the middle.

The Maker can likewise slice up to three layers of light cotton simultaneously, along these lines making uniform cuts so a lot simpler!

One all the more way the Cricut Maker can cut unexpected materials in comparison to the Explore Air 2, Explore Air and Explore is a direct result of the blade sharp edge. The blade sharp edge likewise implies it does a superior and increasingly exact activity of cutting those things.

The blade sharp edge is an extra-profound slicing blade that travels through thick materials up to 2.4mm (3/32") thick. That sounds too meager, yet it's definitely not. Think calfskin, overwhelming cardboard, various layers of thick texture and the sky is the limit from there!

For reference, standard notice board is 0.3mm thick. The Cricut Maker can slice through a strong bit of material that is the thickness of eight bits of publication board stacked together!

The blade edge can be contrasted with to a computerized X-Actoblade due to its accuracy and sharpness.

That implies this uncommon sharp edge can slice through balsa wood, mat board and heavier cowhides.

The blade bladecan even slice through kevlar!

What can the Cricut Maker do that a Cricut Explore Air 2, Explore Air and Explore One can't do?

I know this has been in part shrouded in the contrast between a Cricut Explore and a Cricut Maker? Area. I just idea it is smarter to develop it here after I secured why the Maker can cut various materials.

Here are arrangements of every individual cutting machine and its essential abilities:

1. What can the Cricut Maker do?

- Cut and score created materials.
- Compose with no connectors or extra buys.
- Interface with Bluetooth remote innovation.
- Perform with up to 2x quicker cutting and composing.
- Use 10x more capacity to cut hundreds a greater number of materials than some other Cricut cutting machine.
- Utilize a revolving edge for texture cutting.
- Use a blade to slice and cut through thicker materials.
- Utilize the Scoring Wheel instruments for extremely sharp creases.
- Cut out sewing designs.

2. What can a Cricut Explore Air 2 do?

- Cut and score created materials.
- Compose with no connectors or extra buys.

- Interface with Bluetooth remote innovation or with a rope.
- Perform with up to 2x quicker cutting and composing.

3. What can a Cricut Explore Air do?
- Cut and score create materials.
- Compose with no connectors or extra buys.
- Associate with Bluetooth remote innovation or with a line.

4. What can a Cricut Explore One do?
- Cut and score create materials.
- Compose, however just with the acquisition of the Accessory Adapter.
- Interface with Bluetooth, however just with the acquisition of a remote connector.

As a scrapbooker or side interest crafter, finding a shaper that enables you to investigate your enthusiasm can help support your certainty and profitability. Discussing cutters, Cricut is one of only a handful hardly any organizations that have totally beyond words make. Be that as it may, as you probably are aware, no a few machine models are the very same (regardless of whether they originate from a similar organization). Along these lines, here is our input on which model meets all requirements to be known as the Best Cricut Machine dependent on highlights and audits.

Six Different Models With There Pros/Cons And Verdicts

A must-have gadget for any specialist needing to spare time on their ventures, Cricut machines empower you to decisively cut a huge scope of different material sorts, delivering incredible outcomes each time. The best Cricut machine will offer an addition of sizes for slicing purposes and permit you to play out the undertaking on more than 100 or more material decisions, for example, vinyl, felt, card, cowhide, and even channel tape. With going with programming as standard, you can cut, compose, and score to create slick and expert outcomes inevitably.

This devoted survey takes an inside and out take a gander at six of the top of the line Cricut machines. Concentrating on those highlights here, for example, the size of the machine, serviceable materials, composing and scoring potential outcomes nearby remote choices, we likewise feature some other advantages worth referencing. Wrapping up each component, we offer a little projectile rundown of aces and any potential cons, as well.

By examining the market, we've had the option to put our discoveries into a table and audit them in detail, furnishing you with a last evaluating and differences for each model. Putting together our work with respect to broad inspecting information, we likewise present an accommodating purchasing guide which clarifies those highlights featured in somewhat more detail. At long last, we answer a portion of those most ordinarily suggested conversation starters about these machines. With this data consolidated, when you come to buy the best model for your needs, you'll have the option to choose the best Cricut machine with complete certainty.

1. Cricut Cuttlebug

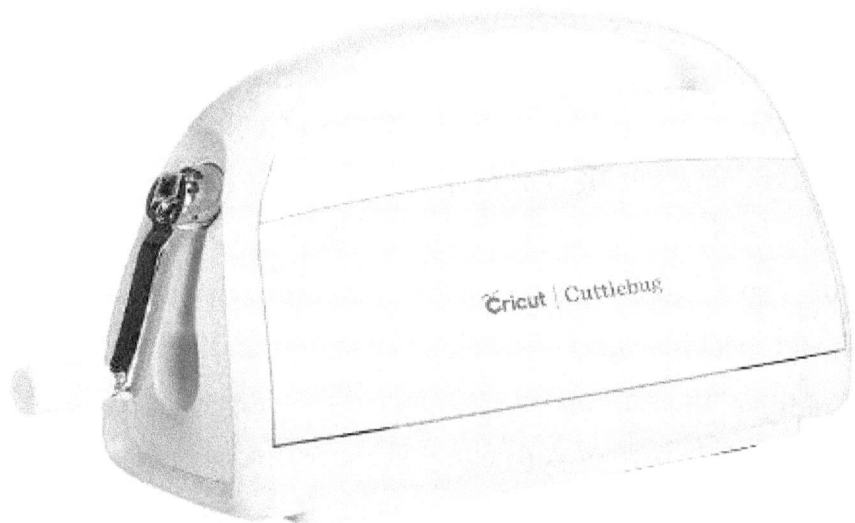

The Cricut Cuttlebug is a Budget pick and maybe the best Cricut machine for fledglings. A most minimized plan, it flaunts everything that you have to begin. This comes total with an A Plate and two B plates and an elastic emblazoning mat. As a little something extra, you'll likewise discover an A2 emblazoning envelope and two metal bites the dust.

This model is perfect for getting together and taking out in a hurry, such is its compactable crease and store plan – just as its collapsible handle highlight. In spite of the fact that it might be little in stature, it can at present slice through a wide assortment of materials – from foil and tissue paper to acetic acid derivation lace and even flimsy cowhide. Be that as it may, it's most huge preferred position here is that it can emblazon – one of the main Cricut machines to do as such!

This implies proficient looking outcomes each time with even and clean decorating giving profound and fresh cuts unfailingly. In addition, this model can likewise work with other driving embellishing cutting kicks the bucket and envelopes. One of the most effortless of Cricut machines to work this is an altogether physically worked machine and hence requires no attachments or leads. Direct to utilize, it offers solid suction and is maybe the best decision of low-tech Cricut machines available. This is ideal for adding surface and additional measurements to numerous undertakings.

Clients of the Cricut Cuttlebug discover this completely down to earth while shipping, just as making it simpler to make on. Having the option to emblazon on such a littler and less expensive machine likewise rates exceptionally with many fulfilled clients.

Pros

- Just Cricut model to decorate!
- Little and compactable
- Incredible for going with
- Requires no links or associations
- Simple to utilize immediately
- Ease

- **Cons**
  - Most appropriate for card making ventures
  - Manual plan
  - Restricted highlights

2. Cricut Explore Air

The Explore air is one more extraordinary section level Cricut machine for apprentices that takes into account tweaked plans. It incorporates all that you may need to make shocking DIY ventures and specialties. Like the Explore One, it likewise cuts a wide assortment of materials with sublime exactness. From thick textures like cowhide to paper, adhesive vinyl, vellum, and even iron-on, it definitely cuts more than 60 sorts of materials.

In contrast to the Explore One, this machine has double carriage including one for a shaper and the other one for a marker. This essentially implies it can without much of a stretch cut a card and compose a tweaked message on the card in one stage. Additionally, it can cut a crate and afterward score its overlay lines all the while. Also, the double apparatus holder helps keep your pen and edge consistently inside reach.

Notwithstanding that, it comes coordinated with a Bluetooth work for quick and remote cutting. Thusly, you can associate the machine to your tablet, work area or cell phone and control it without the requirement for links or wires. You can likewise send every one of your specialties and ventures remotely to the gadget for cutting.

In addition, the gadget is fitted with the simple to-utilize Design Space programming that is perfect with almost all Android and iOS gadgets, and Mac and Windows PCs. The product empowers you to get to a large number of text styles and pictures for nothing or at a little charge.

Further, the Explore Air incorporates the well-known Smart Set dial capacity to assist you with making multifaceted cuts or make custom settings for different materials. Because of its Cut Smart innovation, making clean cuts of a wide range of sizes and shapes is likewise simple.

Another extraordinary element of this machine is that it bolsters all Cricut cartridges.

In that capacity, you can make various kinds of cards in a moment and without agonizing such a great amount over the plan. Additionally, the gadget gives you the alternative of transferring your own arrangement of pictures in different configurations like .jpg, .gif, .png, .svg, .dxf, and .bmp.

Like the Explore One machine, it likewise accompanies more than 50 free tasks and 100 pictures alongside a beginning aide. You will likewise get an iron-on and cardstock test so you have a simple time making your first artworks. Additionally included with the buy is a metallic silver pen to assist you with adding wonderful embellishments to your activities so they stand apart from the rest.

As though that is insufficient, the Explore Air packs a top notch German carbide sharp edge intended to slice through both light and medium-weight materials precisely. Other than that, it accompanies worked away compartments for putting away your apparatus securely and advantageously. Different frill included with the buy are standard hold cutting mat, power line, embellishment connector, and USB line.

Pros

- Cuts and writes in only a solitary advance
- Well-made with sturdy sharp blades, simple to set up and use
- Supports cartridges
- Overly helpful and simple to utilize iPad application

- Incorporates orange matrix lines to guarantee structures remain focused
- Supports remote cutting

Cons

- Possibly works if there is a web association
- Structure programming is somewhat moderate

3. Cricut Expression 2

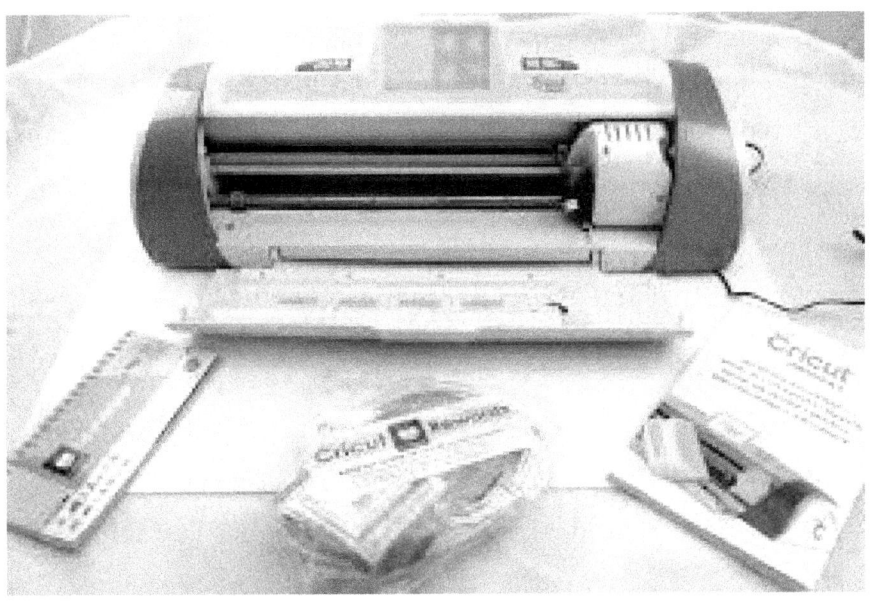

This is an enjoyment machine. Other than that, it's adequately amazing importance you can utilize it for every single fundamental assignment. Nonetheless, it's absolutely cartridge based and that implies it's difficult to utilize it for uniquely crafted structures.

All things considered, it accompanies a full-shading LCD TouchScreen which empowers you to move and even control pictures. In addition, you can utilize it to interface on the web so you can get to the advantages of the Craft Room Software program. This product program contains a great many pictures which you can read and use for bite the dust cutting.

As should be obvious, this is an amazingly simple to-utilize machine. You can agree to it in case you're inexperienced with visual depiction and stuff. For this situation, you'll should simply choose and plug the correct cartridges into the machine. You would then be able to move the structures around and even resize them.

Past that, you can generally utilize the auto-fill choice which once chose empowers you to duplicate the shapes onto the mat on various occasions. That is simply however a scrap of a portion of the efficient highlights this machine accompanies.

Pros

- Incredible efficient plan
- Access to free plans on Craft Room programming
- Capacity to deal with various materials (chipboard, balsa wood, froth, etc.)
- Supported by a 1-year guarantee

Cons

- Restricted visual communication opportunity

4. Cricut Explore One

If you are simply beginning in making and searching for a dependable machine, this is one of the alternatives worth investigating. It looks a great deal like the Explore Air 2 yet they are not the equivalent. Obviously, the Explore One was simply discharged as a cheap option in contrast to the Explore Air 2.

Contrasted with the Explore Air 2, Explore One doesn't have Bluetooth innovation. Fortunately you can include a remote Bluetooth connector for remote cutting with your iPhone, PC, iPad, and Mac. In any case, the connector is sold independently.

Be that as it may, most likely the best thing about the machine is that it can cut a wide exhibit of materials. Specifically, you can utilize it to cut vinyl, paper, calfskin, texture, cardstock and even publication board for DIY ventures.

What's more, on account of its Smart Set dial work, the machine enables you to get exact cuts on practically any material. You can also structure a custom setting for a wide assortment of materials. Notwithstanding that, it highlights one of a kind Cut Smart innovation intended to assist you with making clean cuts of various shapes and sizes.

Moreover, the gadget utilizes a German carbide sharp edge that furnishes speedy cut on most textures with incredible exactness. As though that is insufficient, the Explore One underpins cartridges which is the thing that makes it increasingly congenial for fledglings. The cartridges make it simple for anybody to get acquainted with different materials and styles of making.

Proceeding onward, the machine flaunts simple to-utilize and free Design Space programming that is just accessible on the web. This product gives you access to your undertakings and pictures from any good iPhone, Mac, PC, or iPad. Essentially, the product is cloud-based to guarantee your ventures and structures are matched up over the entirety of your gadgets.

In addition? It incorporates more than 50 free pictures and 25 a single tick extends so you can begin when you buy the machine. All the more along these lines, you can transfer your customized pictures and textual styles for nothing or just browse the picture library. You likewise have the choice to read pre-made tasks for cards, home stylistic theme, scrapbook pages, gatherings, and more to fulfill your making needs.

Likewise included are a standard-Grip cutting mat and capacity compartments for included comfort. With the Explore One, you can make such huge numbers of things including pennants, birthday solicitations, wedding presents, and embellishments. Hence, as far as possible will most likely be your minds.

Pros
- Makes ultra-exact cutting
- Incorporates more than 60,000 plan and undertakings thoughts
- Cuts more than 100 unique kinds of materials including printable pictures
- No mind boggling material settings on account of the Smart-set dial
- Moderately economical and works with Design Space
- Simple to utilize and accompanies a guidance direct
- Enables you to plan your activities on your cell phone, PC or tablet

Cons

- Not inserted with Bluetooth so you should purchase a connector
- Incorporates only a solitary holder so you can't cut and compose at the same time
- Cartridges are very costly

5.Cricut Explore Air 2

Next up we have the Explore Air 2 that is accounted for to be multiple times quicker than the past Explore models. From home stylistic theme to cards and custom shirts, the machine enables you to make staggering DIY extends in not more than minutes. What's more, it cuts more than 100 sorts of materials, for example, claim to fame paper, Iron-on Vinyls, fake cowhide, notice board, cardstock, cement foils, and the sky is the limit from there.

The Explore Air 2, similar to the Explore One and Air, makes mind boggling slices each time on account of its Smart Set Dial work. This capacity enables the machine to make cuts just at the right weight and profundity for a wide range of materials. Furthermore, it incorporates the free Design Space programming that is cloud-based. The product empowers you to alter and redo your undertakings in a hurry.

Furthermore, it includes a double device holder so you can cut and compose or essentially cut and score in a solitary advance. Utilizing the Cricut pens, you can actually make written by hand cards or undertakings utilizing your preferred textual style for nothing. Additionally, you can without much of a stretch make overlap lines for boxes, cards, paper specialties, and envelopes utilizing a scoring stylus.

Another element worth referencing is its worked in Bluetooth availability intended to guarantee quicker remote cutting, scoring, and composing. Therefore, you can send your plans and ventures from your cell phone, PC or tablet to the machine for ideal comfort.

With more than 3,000 pre-made undertakings and plan thoughts to browse, the machine gives you unlimited potential outcomes in the picture library. Plus, you can generally transfer and utilize your picture documents, work of art just as textual styles completely for nothing. As though that is insufficient, the Explore Air 2 empowers you to print full-shading examples or pictures and afterward cut them out.

Proceeding onward, it utilizes Cut Smart innovation for simplicity of making exact cuts. The innovation additionally takes into account easy choice of pre-adjusted materials. All the more in this way, the gadget accompanies a top notch German Carbide sharp edge and works very well with cartridges. However, hold up there is more. The Explore Air 2 packs a cardstock test, standard cutting mat, start manage, more than 50 free venture thoughts, and more than 100 free pictures.

Pros

- Slices effectively through printable pictures
- Simple to-utilize programming
- Slices and reviews to 2X quicker
- Incorporates pictures and a great many plan thoughts for almost every venture
- Flaunts simple material settings
- Lovely and up-to-date plan with vintage hues

Cons

- A few clients have has issues with the product
- Cutting mat loses its clingy exceptionally quick

6. Cricut Maker

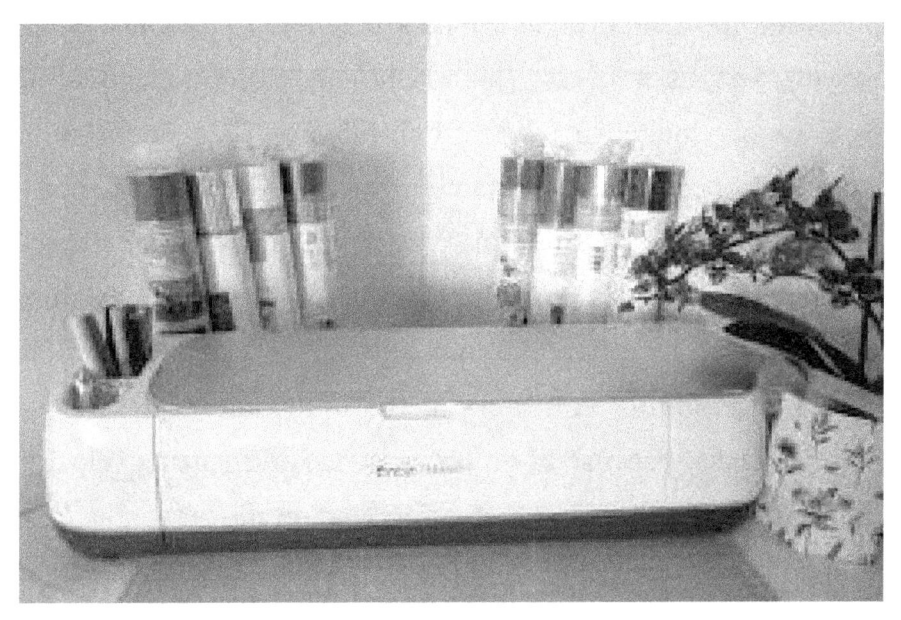

The Cricut Maker makes the highest priority on our rundown, as this is viewed as a definitive in keen cutting machines. It permits the slicing of up to 300 distinct kinds of materials and is quicker when cutting and composing than other Cricut models. With everything incorporated that makes Cricut so mainstream, and substantially more in addition, this is the most expandable machine in the arrangement. Encased here you'll discover incredible blades, a scoring instrument, and pens.

The rotational sharp edge in this machine professes to slice through practically any texture quickly, with the blade edge additionally downplaying most undertakings, all on the two cutting mats notwithstanding. This model has an amazing 50 prepared to-make designs which are generally free, just as 25 sewing designs. Working this machine couldn't be simpler as you simply look over the straightforward plan application, spread it out on your favored gadget and the Cricut denotes every one of the pieces for you. Finding a workable pace cutting, it's ideal for the two amateurs, as your first venture materials are incorporated, and experts, as it is an incredible Cricut machine for educators or the individuals who achieve various tasks, because of its convenience and cutting velocity. You can even utilize your own structures on the off chance that you'd like. Besides, this machine is intended to hold your cell phone or tablet, permitting you to charge such gadgets through its USB port, or associate remote through its Bluetooth innovation.

Clients of the Cricut Maker exceptionally rate its convenience, however its capacity to offer unlimited conceivable outcomes when slicing through even the hardest of materials, yet still

Pros

- Exceptionally incredible cutting sharp blades
- Well-evaluated at an under $500 sticker price
- Accompany a rich sewing library

- This is a genuine work-horse with a turbocharged motor
- Has an incredible and blade plan
- Robotized innovation which identifies whether you're utilizing the right sharp edge or not

Cons
- The cutting space is still very constrained
- Still uses the online Design Space programming

Purchasing Guide

Presently you've gotten an opportunity to glance through our surveys on these five fabulous models, you may have a superior thought of the best Cricut machine that would suit your needs. However, before you settle on that last obtaining choice, investigate the accompanying purchasing guide. This short yet instructive area extends somewhat more on a portion of the highlights we referenced previously. This will assist you with ensuring that you get all the basic advantages from your ideal Cricut model and can determine the most use out of it for some brilliant years to come.

Cricut compared with its opposition: what are the focal points?

There are a couple of contender models out there available, yet up 'til now nothing rivals a Cricut machine.

In spite of the fact that a few people may feel the cost of the Cricut is maybe the greatest concern, you unquestionably get what you pay for with these models. That equivalents an extraordinary industry most loved which can cut like no other machine can, access to many activities all from the one model, and creating which is such a great amount of enjoyment all the while.

The plans of Cricut machines, in any event, offering stockpiling arrangements, are professed to be the most streamlined and subsequently down to earth. The product that is incorporated as standard here is said to be the best available and permits more critical potential outcomes and decision than different models. It's additionally the simpler to transfer and make a record for just as permitting clients to transfer their own one of a kind pictures and plans on the off chance that they want to.

Besides, these machines are tough and sturdy, serving numerous clients for quite a while, bother free.

Highlights to consider before purchasing a Cricut machine

Before you choose the best model for you, you might need to consider a portion of the standard and extra highlights that a Cricut machine can offer you.

This can incorporate different cutting paces, fluctuated material settings, extra instruments, expanded scoring and composing capacities, various modifications and settings, remote ability, and even apparatus holders on the model itself.

Cutting velocity

Most Cricut machines will work at quick standard velocities, however there are more current models, for example, the Cricut Maker or Cricut Explore Air 2, which offer significantly quicker cutting occasions, as much as up to multiple times that of the standard models. Nonetheless, a sped up won't modify the impacts of your ventures or change the outcomes – it simply implies that you can accomplish more with hardly a pause in between.

Note: *A quicker machine will possibly truly be valuable to you in the event that you have to get past a great deal in one session, or in the event that you use it all the time for various activities, maybe even some expert.*

Materials you can work with

All Cricut machines permit you to take a shot at a wide scope of material decisions. In any case, you if have a particular material as a top priority, you should twofold check the determination on your chose model to guarantee it can adapt to that specific sort.

Good blades and pens Each Cricut machine will have a choice of blades that are generally perfect with your gadget.

From premium fine focuses, profound focuses, rotating blades, blade sharp blades, and reinforced textures to scoring wheels, when you do purchase a substitution, you should ensure that the model indicated on the blade bundling is perfect with your model number.

A similar guidance applies to Cricut pens. You should guarantee they are additionally perfect with your model. This is on the grounds that most pens are made expressly for explicit machines and accordingly won't fit any others.

Note: *Take care to read the detail on your substitution pens before acquiring them.*

Scoring and composing capacities

The composing capacity of a Cricut machine will permit you to use the Cricut pens and produce transcribed style cards and ventures. It will do this through the textual styles that are on offer in the machine or by those you can access through download. You just select the textual style, at that point kick back and watch it compose! With respect to the scoring component, this is the part that makes those ideal crease lines, envelopes, cards, 3D paper specialties, boxes, acetic acid derivation pinwheels, and substantially more other than.

Depth and pressure adjustment

The profundity and weight modification on your Cricut machine will decide how well the material that you picked is cut.

It's hence fundamental to guarantee you select the correct setting for every material you place in the machine to get those best of results. In this way, in case you're cutting thicker material, the weight and profundity will be something contrary to what you would utilize in the event that you were cutting card – and the other way around.

A couple of hardware holders

Apparatus holders are helpful when situated on the Cricut machine as they permit you to store your devices while you work. This implies they are close by at whatever point you're taking a shot at a venture and kept securely out of damage's way. Having a devoted space for your devices can keep you from losing them or losing them as you work and it can likewise draw out their life expectancy as they're shielded from your other hardware. Some Cricut machines offer one apparatus holder, some offer two. The number might be increasingly close to home inclination and with respect to what number of devices you're taking a gander at holding or putting away as you take a shot at your machine.

Remote capacities

If your Cricut machine is remote the conceivable outcomes of finding a large number of more plans and on various gadgets is expanded enormously. A portion of the Cricut models might be empowered remotely with utilization of a connector, for example, the Cricut Explore One.

Where others, for example, the Cricut Explore Air 2 have implanted Bluetooth which makes them right away remote without the need to buy and utilize extra things. In case you're quick to utilize your Cricut through different gadgets around the home, a remote model will be tremendously down to earth for you.

Software you can use to make your structures

Cricut offers standard basic structure programming to all buyers of Cricut models. This is free for all clients to get to. Furthermore, you can utilize this product on an assigned application and work from your telephone or introduce the product on numerous gadgets, from PCs to tablets. The product expects to permit you to redo, alter and review your tasks. You can decide to do this both on the web and disconnected, as the new disconnected highlights permit access without a web association.

Suggestions on the most proficient method to set up and utilize a Cricut machine

It truly couldn't be any simpler to set up and utilize your Cricut machine. The first occasion when you start your machine, you'll be incited to naturally enlist the gadget to your record. You do this by turning it on, interfacing the Cricut to your PC, and getting to the arrangement connect given in your guidance manage.

This will lead you through a progression of guidelines where you will be incited to make a Cricut ID. Here, you would then be able to download and introduce the module required and afterward get straight onto that first task!

Utilizing the machine is similarly as direct. You place the instrument you need into the cartridge, space your material determination in, and afterward select the cut you need. The machine at that point finds a good pace for you. It truly is that simple!

Tips

- Care for your slicing mat – Aim to keep it secured with the plastic shield, initially included, on it when not being used. Likewise, give it a wipe consistently to prevent it from encountering material buildups and develop.
- Burden your mat accurately before you start cutting by twofold checking it. The mat needs to slip inside the rollers. On the off chance that it isn't stacked appropriately it will cut each time erroneously. On the off chance that it starts to lose its stick, it might merit putting resources into another one.
- Watch out for your blades and check for indications of inadequacy and bluntness. In the event that your machine isn't carving entirely through, lifts or pulls the vinyl off your support sheet, or is tearing your vinyl and card, you may need to supplant your blades.

- Put resources into a determination of apparatuses to utilize your machine to its latent capacity – But ensure they are the correct devices for the employments you'll likely be embraced the most. A fundamental toolset will as a rule comprise of scrubbers, tweezers, weeding devices, spatulas, and scissors.
- Attempt to test your materials first each time you start with another task. Along these lines you don't get excessively far into the slicing procedure just to acknowledge it isn't exactly working how you initially arranged. This is for the most part a smart thought when utilizing materials, for example, felt and wood and even some master textures.
- Utilize the product included with your machine and exploit the same number of the free pictures, textual styles and structures as you can. These can regularly help with launching numerous new ventures and acquainting you with parts of the machine you may never have considered.

Cricut Explore Review

A Closer Look at the Cricut Explore Family

The Cricut Explore One is the shaper that carried a significant distinction to the universe of specialty cutting. It's an entirely fundamental machine and is, along these lines, suggested for tenderfoots. The second individual from the family, the Explore Air, went under the spotlight in 2015. Truth be told, it was among the initial ones to present remote cutting ability. That is on the grounds that it accompanied Bluetooth availability which wasn't accessible on the Explore One item. The most up to date kid on the square, the Cricut Explore Air 2, was propelled in 2016 with the expectation of ousting the Silhouette Cameo 3 from the best work area create shaper position.

One of a kind trait of the Explore line of items is that they're essentially valued. They're additionally very simple to-utilize and appear to be essentially intended for amateurs and specialists.

Yet, obviously, after some time, Cricut has attempted to present a couple of more highlights no matter how you look at it. In this way, for example, the Explore Air 2 has a larger number of highlights than Explore One, etc. Sounds like a serious piece? Indeed, how about we investigate what each model accompanies.

Cricut Explore One

In case you're searching for a specialty shaper that is sufficiently simple to ace, the Cricut Explore One would be an incredible fit. Retailing at just underneath $200, this DIY machine flaunts exact cutting, scoring, and composing innovation. Other than that, it includes the capacity to cut many various materials.

Hoping to cut examples or pictures that are in your telephone with a kick the bucket shaper? The Explore One has got you secured. It accompanies an inviting interface which permits you to effortlessly structure your venture even by SmartPhone, PC, or tablet.

Other than that, when you request a bit of it, you'll likewise get 60,000+ venture and plan thoughts. You can utilize those to fuel up your imaginative vocation at no extra expense. Usually, different organizations expect you to buy venture and plan thoughts independently however Cricut spares you that cost.

In addition? This machine is a brute of sorts as it's fit for cutting various materials running from cowhide to vinyl. This is on account of the way that it incorporates German carbide premium sharp edge. This is a ground-breaking blade that is intended to slice light-to mid-weight items. Other than that, the sharp edge is profoundly flexible to wear and breakage which gives it a long life.

All things considered, the Explore One comes up short on the capacity to work remotely.

It doesn't accompany an implicit Bluetooth usefulness importance you'd have to interface links to move pictures.

Key Features

1. Smart Set Dial

This is a creative material choice element. It accompanies foreordained settings which assist you with getting ideal outcomes as long as you work the machine on the correct mode. The beneficial thing with this element is that it takes out the need to alter speed, profundity, and weight physically.

2. Integrated Storage Compartments

These compartments are inventively intended to suit however much of your work things as could reasonably be expected. In case you're hoping to keep your office mess free, these eventual extraordinary space savers.

3. Cricut Design Space Software

This is an exceptionally ground-breaking programming that can be gotten to by means of either an iPhone, iPad, Android, Windows or Mac PCs. You just need to sign in to the framework and you'll discover many ravishing pre-made tasks. That implies you can choose from a huge number of instant tasks. What's more, the most delightful piece of this Design Space programming is that you just need to choose and tap the "Make It Now" button. Along these lines, this is an exceptionally clear item to utilize.

4. StandardGrip Cutting Mat

This slicing mat has been tweaked to suit various types of making materials. They have an incredible grasp and gloat the capacity to hold the material immovably set up making it simple to expel the material. This multipurpose mat is of high caliber and flaunts the capacity to make all around flawless cuts.

Pros

- Exceptionally simple to utilize
- Has every one of the rudiments an amateur may require
- Can even now utilize a portion of your old cartridges
- Incredible incentive for cash
- Simple to-utilize Smart Dial to take out the requirement for manual alterations

Cons

- Needs remote innovation
- Can't cut and compose simultaneously

Cricut Explore Air

The Explore Air has everything Explore One has, in addition to a few. For example, it gloats Bluetooth network which implies you use it remotely. This is an incredible element particularly for the individuals who like to configuration utilizing their telephones. Similarly, the remote innovation expels the requirement for links. This goes far in helping keep your workspace clean.

Other than that, the Explore Air accompanies a Double device holder. What's that? You may be pondering. Indeed, the twofold instrument holder gives you the opportunity to cut and compose simultaneously. You, along these lines, don't need to buy an instrument connector for the Explore Air.

On the flipside, however, the machine comes up short on the rotating blade. As you probably are aware, the turning edge is most appropriate for a wide range of texture. An absence of it, along these lines, is a serious deal particularly for those searching for an expert use machine.

We likewise don't care for the way that it doesn't have a blade edge. As you most likely are aware, this sort of blade proves to be useful in cutting thicker materials. In this way, while the Cricut Explore AIR is an extraordinary DIY machine, it is most appropriate for scrapbooking and other light making obligations.

Key Features

1. .SVG, .GIF and .DXF Files Accepted

This reduced machine acknowlblades .jpg, .png and .bmp records yet .dxf and .svg too. Along these lines, you don't need to be left with one record group. As a creator, that is the sort of opportunity you have to stretch your inventiveness as far as possible.

2. Cut Smart Technology

Have you at any point wished to get a machine that would permit you to make exact slices from a quarter-inch to 23.5-inches? This is the place the Cut Smart Technology which is licensed to Cricut proves to be useful. The inventive innovation works through a half breed engine framework intended to improve blade control. At the point when combined up with the Smart Set dial highlight, you appreciate significantly more prominent authority over the sorts of cuts you can deal with at some random minute.

3. iPad App

Notwithstanding its remote usefulness, this machine can likewise be worked through an iPad application. Along these lines, you can deal with every one of your plans on the telephone and in a hurry. For example, you can exploit those extended periods of time in the metro, holding up in line, going via plane, etc. to deal with your structures. At that point send the plans to the shaper when you're back in your office. Along these lines, in addition to the fact that this helps make the machine advantageous to have around spares your time.

Pros

- Can be worked remotely
- Easy to use and instinctive programming
- Very simple to set up
- Can accomplish such a great deal and even compose utilizing pens
- No product download is required

- Accompanies a helpful iPad application
- Can at present use cartridges however it doesn't require them

Cons

- The Design Space programming must be gotten to on the web
- Somewhat costly contrasted with the Explore One

Cricut Explore Air 2

Of the three machines from Cricut that bear the name "Investigate" the Explore Air 2 is, no uncertainty, the best. Far beyond every one of the highlights the Explore One and Explore Air accompany, this one accompanies a twofold instrument holder and 2X quicker cutting force.

As should be obvious from that rundown of extra highlights, the Air 2 is intended to convey more force. Along these lines, in case you're hoping to grow your vocation, this would be an ideal decision. Additionally, in the event that you've been battling to comply with work time constraints, the additional speed will prove to be useful.

Searching for assortment? The Air 2 items extend includes cherry bloom, matte dark, rose group and mint shading variations. Along these lines, you can generally coordinate the machine with different apparatuses in your office. Hi, extraordinary style!

Back to usefulness, this machine accompanies a 3-month enrollment membership to Cricut's superior highlights. Other than that, you get a solid grasp mat, light hold mat, additional top notch sharp edge, advanced cartridges, friends through correspondence textual style and lipstick lettering textual style. How cool is that? Furthermore, there's additional.

This DIY cutting machine accompanies a large number of pre-made plans. Thus, you'll have all the opportunity you have to settle on educated choices consistently. Actually, you have the opportunity to pick between promptly accessible instant layouts or uniquely crafted plans which you can make utilizing the simple to-utilize programming.

In staying aware of the customs of the Explore product offering, this one also has a Smart Set Dial which guarantees that your machine is flexible. Along these lines, you can generally cause the ideal slice since you can pick the sort of profundity and strain to apply.

Proceeding onward, this machine furnishes you with astounding cutting width. The shaper is 12-inches wide and 24-inches in length. That means generally about 11.5-inches and 23.5-inches worth of cutting width. This may not be the biggest cutting limit accessible yet it ought to be sufficient for most making assignments.

To summarize it, the Air 2 appreciates Bluetooth availability, auto-settings, and double carriage usefulness.

In this way, unmistakably, this machine goes well beyond the challenge regarding flexibility and cutting force.

Key Features

1. Bluetooth Wireless Technology

This is likely probably the coolest component to have been presented by Cricut. In case you're similar to a dominant part of scrapbooking fans and DIY devotees, you most likely are battling with mess as of now. The exact opposite thing you need to do is present more mess. Enter Bluetooth innovation and you currently have the opportunity to convey incredible cuts, remotely. Obviously, this innovation possibly works when you're close to the printer however it positively helps a great deal. Truth be told, it rearranges the establishment procedure more than ever.

2. 2X Cutting Speed

Speed is a major issue with regards to the utilization of kick the bucket cutters. What's more, since time is cash, you need to ensure you're doing everything inside your way to spare it. With two fold the amount of cutting force as the Cricut Explore Air this appears to be an ideal counterpart for the bustling crafter. You can really utilize it to begin a private venture in spite of the fact that, obviously, it may not be sufficiently amazing to deal with rock solid business work.

In such manner, you possibly need to choose the Fast Mode when you have to make the most of consistently.

Else, you can utilize the typical mode in case you're not in a hurry to complete things.

3. Free Fonts

Why pay for premium textual styles when you can get them for nothing from Cricut? All things considered, the moment you get an Air 2 for yourself, Penpals Font and Lipstick Lettering Font will be benefited to you at no additional expense. The Penpals textual style is incredible for fun loving plans while the lipstick lettering textual style proves to be useful when strength is required. Additionally, you can even make your very own textual style and transfer it to the framework. Would you be able to envision making your specially crafted textual style and really utilizing it on the entirety of your imaginative tasks? All things considered, the Air 2 is maybe the best arrangement you can ever snatch particularly in case you're hoping to use your inventive juice.

Cricut Explore One versus Cricut Explore Air versus Cricut Explore Air 2

We'd prescribe going for the Explore One in case you're totally new to die-cutting. In case you're a specialist who's hoping to appreciate scrapbooking with the opportunity of wireless connectivity, the Explore Air would be your most logical option.

The Cricut Explore Air 2 proves to be useful when speed is required. In this way, you get additionally slicing force in addition to the opportunity to pick the sort of speed you need your specialties made at.

Last Thoughts

As should be obvious, the Cricut Explore product offering presents a wide assortment of choices. You should simply comprehend your one of a kind needs and go for the shaper that best addresses your issues. Some of the time, you should simply discover one that falls inside your financial limit. In any case, on the off chance that you're considering going completely proficient, at that point getting a machine with extra-cutting rate and force may be the best activity.

Chapter Two

How to Use Cricut Machine (Cricut Expression 2)

We're presenting something exceptionally extraordinary — the Cricut Expression 2 machine. It's an all-new form of the Cricut Expression Personal Electronic Cutter. Outwardly, we've given it an all-new look, including a full-shading LCD contact screen that is greater and quicker. Within, all the incredible highlights of the Cricut Expression machine has been kept, and numerous extraordinary new highlights has been included.

Your Cricut Expression 2 machine will do everything Cricut Expression machine will do and has:

• A mat review which enables you to see shapes you're cutting and where they fit on the mat before you cut.

• All new materials settings, enabling you to pick a default setting for materials you like to cut like cardstock or chipboard, or modify a material setting to be exactly how you need it.

• A slicing region light to let you see where you're cutting on the mat.

• Independent picture estimating enabling you to measure each picture on a mat without anyone else. Make one picture 3" and another picture 5 ½" — all on a similar mat.

• Multiple mat cutting so you can cut the same number of pictures as you need, regardless of whether the pictures won't all fit on one mat. Your Cricut Expression 2 activities can contain up to six mats.

DIAGRAMS

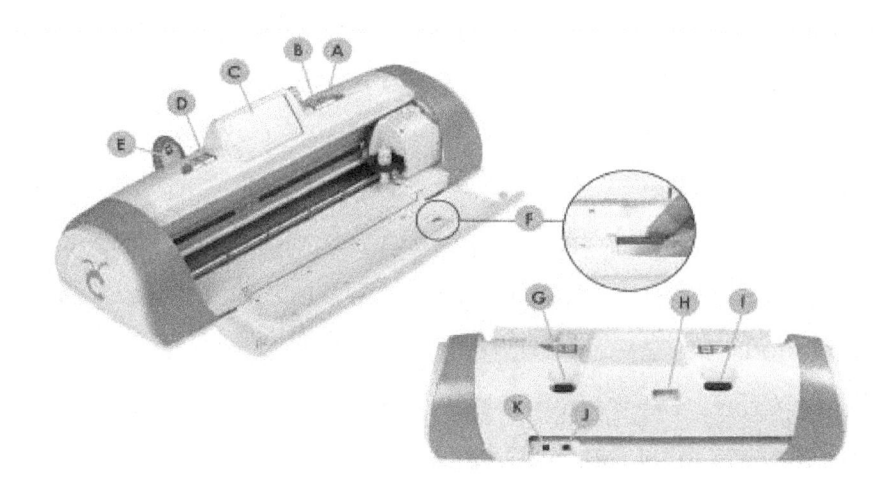

A	On Button
B	**PAUSE** Button
C	Touch Screen
D	Home Button
E	Zoom Button
F	Stylus
G	Cricut Imagine® Cartridge Port
H	Wifi Port
I	Original Cricut® Cartridge Port
J	USB Port
K	Power Cable Port

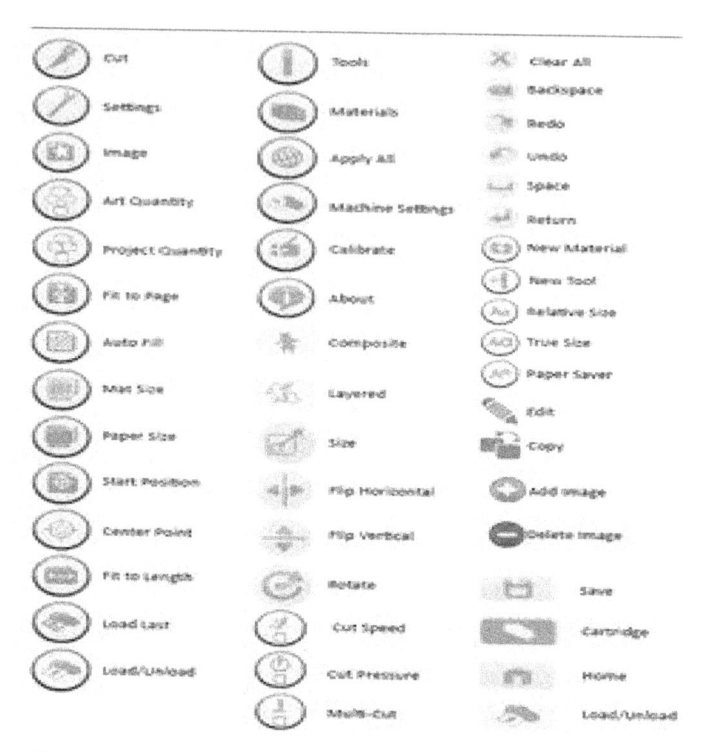

⊘	Cut	①	Tools	✕	Clear All
⊘	Settings	▨	Materials		Backspace
	Image	⊚	Apply All		Redo
	Art Quantity		Machine Settings		Undo
	Project Quantity		Calibrate		Space
	Fit to Page		About		Return
	Auto Fill		Composite		New Material
	Mat Size		Layered		New Tool
	Paper Size		Size		Relative Size
	Start Position		Flip Horizontal		True Size
	Center Point		Flip Vertical		Paper Saver
	Fit to Length		Rotate		Edit
	Load Last		Cut Speed		Copy
	Load/Unload		Cut Pressure		Add Image
			Multi-Cut		Delete Image
					Save
					Cartridge
					Home
					Load/Unload

Security Information

Separate electrical force before adjusting or cleaning.

Caution! Try not to put your fingers or different articles in the Cricut Expression 2 machine while it is associated with electrical force, controlled on, or during cutting activities. Fast developments of the cutting carriage during activity may cause substantial damage or potentially harm to the Cricut Expression 2 machine.

Continuously follow fundamental security precautionary measures when utilizing this item to diminish danger of damage from fire or electric stun. Read and see all directions in the documentation that accompanies the Cricut Expression 2 machine.

Watch all alerts and directions set apart on the item.

Try not to introduce or utilize this item close to water or when you are wet. Introduce the item safely on a steady surface.

Introduce the item in a secured area where nobody can step on or stumble over the force line and the force string can't be harmed.

If the item doesn't work regularly, see troubleshooting.

There are no client useful parts inside. Allude adjusting to qualified assistance faculty.

The force rope can't be fixed. If it is imperfect, it ought to be disposed of or came back to the provider.

Ozone-exhausting synthetic concoctions, for example, chlorofluorocarbons (CFCs), have been killed from the Provo Craft fabricating forms.

This item contains lead in the weld that may require exceptional taking care of at end-of-life.

FCC Statement

The U.S. Government Communications Commission (in 47 cfr 15.105) has indicated that the accompanying notification be brought to the consideration of clients of this item.

This gadget conforms to section 15 of the FCC rules. Activity is dependent upon the accompanying two conditions: (1) this gadget may not cause hurtful obstruction, and (2) this gadget must acknowledge any impedance got, including obstruction that may cause undesired activity.

Protected Cables

Utilization of a protected information link is required to agree to the Class B cutoff points of Part 15 of the FCC Rules.

As per part 15.21 of the fCC runs, any progressions or adjustments to this gear not explicitly endorsed by provo Craft may cause hurtful obstruction and void the fCC approval to work this hardware.

Note: this gear has been tried and found to conform as far as possible for a Class B computerized gadget, as per Part 15 of the FCC Rules. These breaking points are intended to give sensible assurance against hurtful obstruction in a private establishment. This hardware creates, utilizes, and can transmit radio recurrence vitality and, if not introduced and utilized as per the guidelines, may make hurtful impedance radio correspondences. In any case, there is no assurance that obstruction won't happen in a specific establishment. If this hardware causes unsafe impedance to radio or TV gathering, which can be controlled by killing the gear and on, the client is urged to attempt to address the obstruction by at least one of the accompanying measures:

- Reorient or migrate the getting radio wire.
- Increase the partition between the hardware and beneficiary.
- Connect the hardware into an outlet on a circuit not quite the same as that to which the beneficiary is associated.
- Consult the vendor or an accomplished radio/T expert for help.

Beginning

Introducing the Cutting Blade Assembly

The Cricut Expression 2 cutting sharp edge gathering is situated in the base of your case, separate from the machine. Before you turn the machine on, you should embed the blade get together. To do this:

1. Open the front entryway on the Cricut Expression 2 machine. Expel the cardboard additions from the two sides of the carriage.

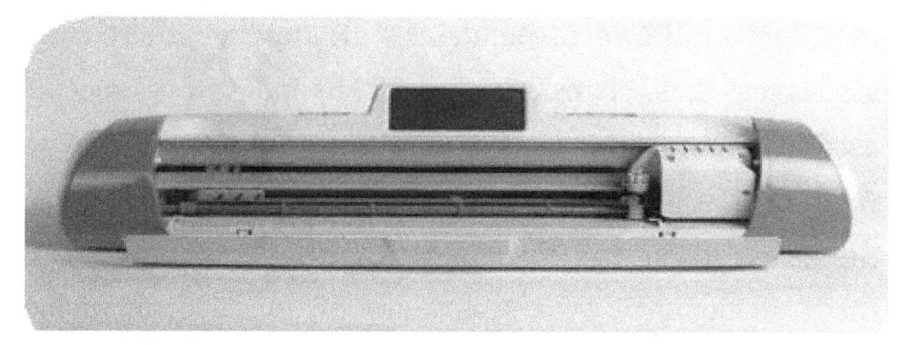

2. Remove the cutting sharp edge get together from its pack. The blade gathering fits into the dark support on the left half of the carriage. Pivot the alteration handle on the highest point of the blade get together so the dark bolt on the edge get together focuses to the number 3 on the change handle.

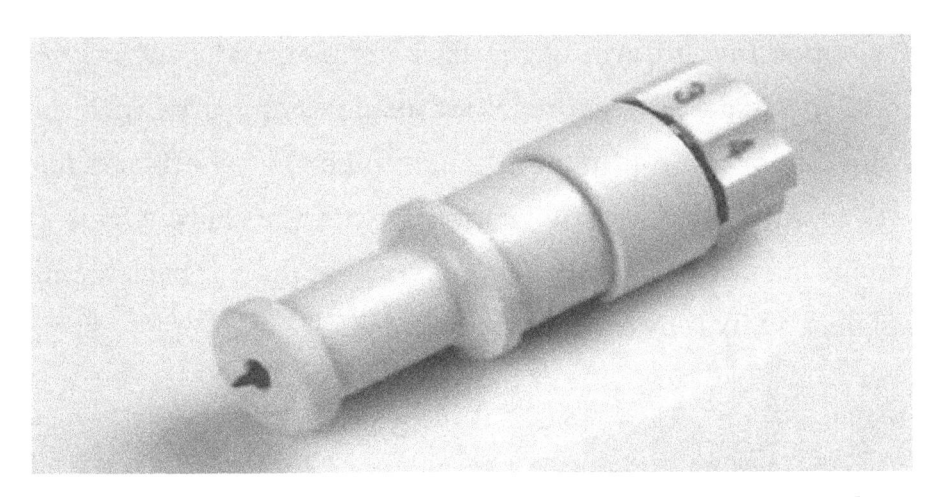

3. Locate the silver nut and turn it counterclockwise until it relaxes enough that you can swing the screw to one side. Be mindful so as not to extricate the screw excessively or it will drop out.

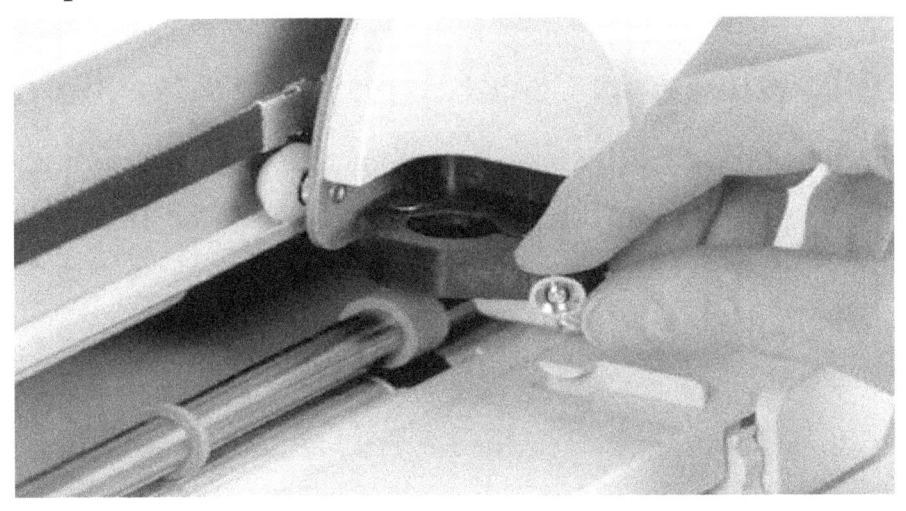

4. Open the left arm of the dark support and position the cutting sharp edge get together inside as appeared with the dark bolt confronting you. Guarantee that the blade has been embedded into the gathering with the sharp edge end pointing down. Close the support, swing the nut back to one side, and fix it by turning it clockwise.

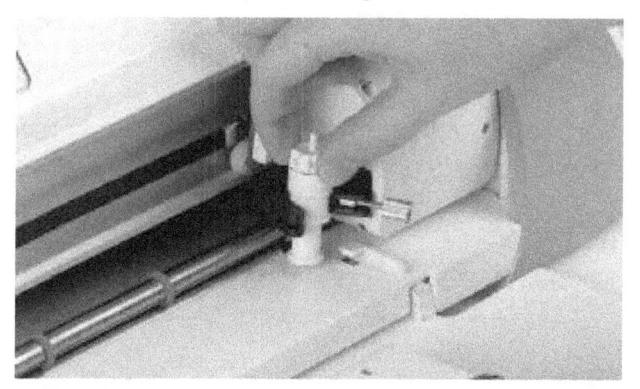

Situating your Cricut Expression 2 Machine

Spot your Cricut Expression 2 machine in any event 12" (30.48 cm) from the edge of your table to keep it from tipping and causing conceivable damage. Permit 24" (60.96 cm) in the rear of the Cricut Expression 2 machine for mat development.

When situating your Cricut Expression 2 machine, pick an area that:

• cannot be gotten to by kids. The Cricut Expression 2 machine isn't a toy and contains parts, including a sharp edge, that could be unsafe to kids.

- is a hard, stable, and level surface inside 6 feet (1.83 meters) of a grounded electrical outlet, and that has a base freedom of 24" (60.96 cm) behind the Cricut Expression 2 machine for paper development.

- is inside or in a dry area where the Cricut® cartridges are not straightforwardly presented with the impacts of the climate.

- is away from direct presentation to daylight or outrageous temperatures, for example, in left vehicles, stockpiling sheds, sunrooms, and so forth.

Caution! Your Cricut Expression 2 machine ought to never be left or put away outside, in areas without warmth or cooling, or in conditions where the machine or cartridges can interact with water. It is suggested that your Cricut Articulation 2 machine be kept up in a territory with temperatures somewhere in the range of 60 and 90 °F (15.5 and 32.2 °C).

Power

Attach the force string into a grounded electrical outlet. Turn the machine on by pressing the force button situated to one side of the screen.

Screen Calibration

Preceding your first utilization of your Cricut Expression 2 machine, it will run a screen adjustment.

Guidelines on the screen will walk you through each progression of the adjustment. You will just need to finish the alignment procedure effectively once. If, for reasons unknown, you wish to recalibrate the machine.

After you complete the screen adjustment, consent to the end client permit understanding, and survey the guarantee data, you will be prepared to start your first task!

First Project

1. On the home screen, press the Image button legitimately to one side of the review mat.

2. Select one of the pictures by pressing the relating button.

3. The picture you chose will be added to the Image Queue.

4. Press the home button situated at the base right of the screen.

5. Press the Cut button situated to one side of the review mat.

6. Remove the reasonable plastic defensive sheet from the cutting mat and mount a 12" x 12" (30.48 cm x 30.48 cm) bit of paper on the mat.

7. Select the material from the dropdown menu that most intently coordinates the paper you mounted on the mat.

8. Verify that the right cutting instrument has been embedded into the machine and has been set to the best possible profundity and press the Cut button.

9. Hold the mat up to the rollers and press the Load button at the base of the screen.

10. Press the Cut button.

11. When the cutting activity closes, press the unload Mat button to discharge the mat from the machine and strip the picture from the mat.

What your Cricut Expression 2 Machine Can Cut

The Cricut Expression 2 machine can cut a wide scope of materials, from vellum and cardstock to publication board and vinyl. The Cricut Expression 2 machine can even cut flimsy chipboard with the utilization of the Multi-Cut capacity.

Tip: the continued cutting of overwhelming materials may decrease the life of your Cricut Expression 2 machine's cutting sharp edge and mat. Substitution mats and blades can be bought anyplace that Cricut items are sold.

Fundamental Operations

Buttons and Machine Controls

Power — kills the machine on and.

Delay — stops the machine while in a cut. Pressing the Pause button again will begin the cutting activity where it was delayed.

Home — opens the Home screen.

Zoom — Press and hold the Zoom button on the machine reassure and afterward contact the picture. To come back to the ordinary view, discharge the Zoom button and tap the screen.

Cartridge Slots — the two cartridge openings give you the capacity to utilize the entirety of your unique Cricut cartridges just as Cricut Imagine cartridges. Every single unique cartridge fit in the left opening, while Imagine cartridges fit in the correct space. It would be ideal if you note that Cricut Imagine Colors and Patterns cartridges contain just shading printing data and no picture data that can be cut, and in this way won't work with the Cricut Expression 2 machine.

USB — this port enable you to interface the Cricut Expression 2 machine to a Gypsy Handheld Design Studio for Cricut or other structure gadget and cut legitimately from that gadget.

Home Screen

The home Screen is your beginning stage for each Cricut Expression 2 undertaking. On this screen you will have the option to see a set of the present venture just as approach picture determination and the capacity to makes changes to cut and different settings.

Mat preview

The **Mat preview** gives a general perspective on your present venture. Each picture that has been added to the task will show up on the mat. Pressing a picture will enable you to make changes to the picture straightforwardly. Pressing the **Edit** symbol will enable you to make changes to the picture itself. Pressing the **Delete** symbol will expel the picture from the venture. Pressing the **Copy** symbol will copy the picture, setting a second duplicate of it to the prompt right of the picture.

If your project contains more than one mat, you can explore among them utilizing the route keys underneath the mat see region.

Mat navigation Keys

Hop First — moves you to the primary mat in the task. If you are presently seeing the primary mat in the task, this button will be turned gray out and inaccessible for choice.

Previous — moves you to the mat legitimately before to the one you are presently seeing. If you are as of now seeing the first mat in the undertaking, this button will be turned gray out and inaccessible for choice.

Page — contains a sign of which mat in the undertaking is at present being shown above, just as a tally of the number of mats contained in the project.

Next— moves you to the mat legitimately after the one that you are at present survey. If you are as of now seeing the last mat in the venture, this button will be turned gray out and inaccessible for determination.

Bounce Last — moves you to the last mat in the venture. If you are at present review the last mat in the undertaking, this button will be turned gray out and inaccessible for choice.

Navigation Buttons

To one side of the Mat Preview zone, there are four route buttons which give access to different elements of the Cricut Expression 2 machine.

Picture Button — Opens the Image Screen, where you can choose pictures, content, symbols, and different components to remember for your venture.

Settings Button — Opens the Settings Screen, where you can control a wide assortment of settings for your task, for example, fit to page and Auto fill.

Cut Button — Opens the Cut Screen, where you can control Cricut Expression 2 settings, for example, the weight and speed of the blade, enter multi-cut choices, just as spare and reuse cutting profiles for materials you work with regularly. Press this button when you are prepared to cut your task.

Load/unload Button — stacks and empties the mat in anticipation of cutting your task.

Picture Screen

The Image Screen is the focal area for choosing and altering pictures you need to remember for your task.

Compatible Cartridges

Your Cricut Expression 2 machine accompanies preloaded inner cartridges. You can likewise utilize any unique Cricut cartridges and Cricut Imagine Art cartridges for Cricut Expression 2 tasks. Cricut Imagine Colors and Patterns cartridges, nonetheless, contain just printing data and consequently can't be utilized with the Cricut Expression 2 machine.

Choosing Cartridges

If you embed a unique cartridge into the Cricut Expression 2 machine, it will consequently be shown in Keypad Mode in the Image Screen. Embedding a Cricut Imagine cartridge without anyone else or alongside a unique cartridge will bring about the Cricut Imagine pictures being naturally shown in Gallery Mode. To change the cartridge pictures which are presently being shown, press the Cartridge button at the base left of the Image Screen and afterward select the cartridge you might want to be shown.

Choosing Images

There are two different ways to see the pictures on your Cricut cartridges: Keypad Mode and Gallery Mode.

Keypad Mode

Keypad Mode includes a lattice of picture keys recognizable to Expression proprietors. To choose a picture to be remembered for your task while in Keypad Mode, just press its button and it will be added to the Image Queue situated at the highest point of the Image Screen.

You can utilize Keypad for all unique and inside cartridges.

Exhibition Mode

Exhibition Mode includes a segment of pictures from your Cricut Imagine cartridge which you can read by contacting a picture and hauling it to one side or right. To choose a picture to be remembered for your task while in Gallery Mode, basically contact the picture, press the green in addition to symbol, and it will be added to the Image Queue. You can utilize Gallery Mode when survey and working with pictures from Cricut Imagine cartridges.

Picture Queue

The Image Queue contains the pictures which make up your present task. They are shown in the request they will be cut on the paper when you start the cutting procedure.

You can explore through the Image Queue either by contacting and hauling the pictures left and right or by utilizing the bolt fastens to one side and right of the Image Queue window.

Erase Image in Queue

To erase a picture which is as of now in the line, press the picture and afterward press the

Erase symbol on the enormous form of the picture.

Duplicating Image in Queue

To copy a picture which is as of now in the line, press the picture and afterward press the Copy symbol on the enormous form of the picture. This will include a second duplicate of the picture legitimately to one side of the primary duplicate in the line.

Alter Image in Queue

To alter a picture which is right now in the line, press the picture and afterward press the Edit symbol on the popup window. This will raise the picture in the Image Editor for you to roll out the ideal improvements.

Zoom Image in Queue

To focus in on a picture in the Image Queue to see a bigger, increasingly definite view, press and hold the Zoom button on the machine reassure and afterward contact the picture.

To come back to the typical view, discharge the Zoom button and tap the screen.

Picture Editor

You can change the size of your picture in the Image Editor. To do as such, press the Size button at the base of the screen.

If you need to modify the size:

1. Select either True Size or relative Size for the picture by pressing the comparing button on the base line. Genuine Size pictures are a fixed range from the highest point of the picture to the base. Relative Size pictures alter the stature of the shape relatively dependent on the tallness of different characters that are from a similar cartridge.

2. Adjust the stature of the picture utilizing the Decrease Value and Increase Value fastens on the top column. You can see the current size in the Size Value box between the two buttons.

When you have rolled out the ideal improvements to the picture size, press the spare button to proceed to the Image Editor. You can drop transforms you have made to the picture size by pressing the Cancel button. In the Image Editor you can roll out extra improvements to the picture size by pressing the Size button. Pressing the home button will return you to the Home screen.

Layered and Composite Images

A few pictures that please the Cricut Imagine Art cartridges are isolated into singular components called layers. This division gives you an extra degree of authority over the size of each layer of the picture in your task. Not exclusively can every one of these layers be independently changed to suit your needs, however they can likewise cut independently.

You can control whether a picture from a Cricut Imagine Art cartridge is cut as a solitary picture or in layers utilizing the Composite and Layered buttons at the base left of the Image Editor. Choosing Composite will make the altered picture be cut as a solitary picture. Choosing Layered will cut each layer of the picture independently.

Note: Selecting to cut a composite picture will cause layers that are completely contained inside another layer to not be cut.

Flip Vertical, flip flat, and pivot these three buttons enable you to change the direction of the chose picture.

Flip Vertical — flips the direction of the whole picture vertically or flips a chose bit of the picture if it has been isolated into layers.

Flip flat — flips the direction of the whole picture on a level plane or flips a chose part of the picture if it has been isolated into layers.

Pivot — turns the whole picture 90 degrees clockwise or turns a chose part of the picture if it has been isolated into layers.

Layered and Composite Images

A few pictures that please the Cricut Imagine Art cartridges are isolated into singular components called layers. This partition gives you an extra degree of command over the size of each layer of the picture in your undertaking. Not exclusively can every one of these layers be independently changed to suit your needs, yet they can likewise cut independently.

You can control whether a picture from a Cricut Imagine Art cartridge is cut as a solitary picture or in layers utilizing the Composite and Layered buttons at the base left of the Image Editor. Choosing Composite will make the altered picture be cut as a solitary picture. Choosing Layered will cut each layer of the picture independently.

Note: Selecting to cut a composite picture will cause layers that are completely contained inside another layer to not be cut.

Flip Vertical, flip flat, and pivot these three buttons enable you to change the direction of the chose picture.

Flip Vertical — Flips the direction of the whole picture vertically or flips a chose segment of the picture if it has been isolated into layers.

Flip even — Flips the direction of the whole picture on a level plane or flips a chose bit of the picture if it has been isolated into layers.

Rotate — Turns the whole picture 90 degrees clockwise or turns a chose bit of the picture on if it has been isolated into layers.

Screen Settings

The screen Settings contains access to an assortment of task settings, enabling you to control the pictures in the undertaking, the size of the paper and mat, just as different settings which influence the elements of the whole Cricut Expression 2 machine.

Like the Home page, you can see a review of your present task in the Mat Preview area. If the undertaking contains more than one page, you can move among the various mats utilizing the route fastens underneath the Mat Preview.

You can likewise tell which of the Settings are as of now actuated by taking a gander at the different fastens in the Settings screen.

Art Quantity

This component can be utilized to Repeat every one of the pictures in your line and limit the measure of paper utilized for the task.

This is frequently helpful when you need a few of each piece of your venture or wish to occupy the vacant space on a page. At the point when you press the Art Quantity button, you will see a popup window containing the Art Quantity controls.

You can change the occasions the pictures are repeated by pressing the Decrease Value and Increase Value buttons, at that point pressing the spare button at the base right corner of the screen. You can drop any progressions you have made by pressing the Cancel button at the base left of the screen. The extra, repeated pictures will be added to the Mat Preview quickly following the chose pictures.

Project Quantity

This component can be utilized to Repeat the whole venture. This is regularly valuable when you have to cut your venture a few times. At the point when you press the task Quantity button, you will see a popup window containing the Project Quantity controls.

You can change the occasions the task is repeated by pressing the Decrease Value and Increase Value buttons, at that point pressing the spare button at the base left corner of the screen. You can drop any progressions you have made by pressing the Cancel button at the base right of the screen.

At the point when you cut an undertaking over and again utilizing this element, you will be incited after each task before proceeding with the following. The most extreme number of times a task can be cut is nine.

Fit to page

The fit to page button changes the size of the pictures in the undertaking to fit the whole page. The Mat Preview gives a visual sign of the size of each picture in the undertaking. To restore the pictures to their typical sizes, press the fit to page button once more.

Auto fill

The capacity of the Auto fill button is like the Art Quantity highlight. In any case, rather than picking a particular number of times to Repeat all the venture craftsmanship, utilizing Auto Fill Repeats the task until the page is full. The extra, repeated pictures are reflected in the Mat Preview. To return to the first, non-repeated pictures, press the Auto fill button once more.

Mat Size

The Mat Size button shows the present mat size being utilized in your task.

If you need to change the mat size, press the Mat Size fasten and choose the ideal mat size. The two potential sizes are 12" x 12" (30.48 cm x 30.48 cm) and 12" x 24" (30.48 cm x 60.96cm). The third button enables you to utilize the more extended 12" x 24" mat in scene direction as opposed to picture. To spare your determination, press the spare button at the base right corner of the screen. You can drop any progressions you have made by pressing the Cancel button at the base left of the screen.

Paper Size

The paper Size button enables you to pick a custom paper size for your undertaking. At the point when you press the paper Size button, you will see a popup window containing the Paper Size controls.

The present width and stature are shown in the containers in the center. to utilize paper which is either more extensive or more, press the comparing Increase button until you arrive at the ideal esteem and afterward press the spare button to spare the changes. To utilize a progressively tight or shorter page, press the comparing Decrease button until you arrive at the ideal worth and afterward pressing the spare button to spare the changes. You can drop the progressions by pressing the Cancel button at the base left of the screen.

Subsequent to adjusting the paper size, you will see the new paper size thought about the Mat Preview in the Settings territory and on the Home page.

Start position

The Start position button enables you to change the area where the blade starts your venture on the page. The shaper starts in the upper left corner of the paper as a matter of course. At the point when you press the Start position button you will see a popup window containing the Start Position controls.

To change the beginning stage, press the Increase and Decrease buttons to pick another beginning stage, at that point press the spare button at the base right corner of the screen. You can drop any progressions you have made by pressing the Cancel button at the base left of the screen. In the wake of adjusting the beginning position, the new beginning point will be thought about the Mat Preview and the pictures in the undertaking will be moved to mirror the new beginning point.

Note: You can change the estimations units used to modify the beginning point to be tenths of inches, quarters of inches, millimeters and centimeters in the machine settings Area. This can help you all the more precisely alter the beginning stage for the blade.

Focus point

The Center point button utilizes the focal point of the picture to find the shape in your undertaking as opposed to the lower left corner of the picture. For example, if you were intending to cut an 8" x 10" photo into an oval, utilizing the Center Point work you could utilize the Start Position capacity to move the shaper to the focal point of the photo and select an oval shape. You could then utilize the Center Point capacity to arrange the focal point of the oval with the focal point of the photo.

If there are various pictures on the mat, they will all be joined utilizing each picture's inside point, making a solitary solid picture to be cut. This alternative isn't accessible for ventures which contain in excess of a solitary page. To restore the pictures to the customary area, press the Center point button once more.

Fit to Length

The fit to Length button enables you to choose a flat size you might want your completed venture to be. At the point when you press the fit to Length button you will see a popup window containing the Fit to Length controls. The present length of the venture is recorded in the middle box. To change the length, press the Increase and Decrease buttons.

At the point when you have entered the ideal length, press the spare button at the base right corner of the screen. You can drop any progressions you have made by pressing the Cancel button at the base left of the screen.

Load Last

Pressing the Load Last button shows that you might want to utilize the extra paper from the last venture for the present task. TheCricut Expression 2 machine monitors what parts of the paper were utilized for the last task. At the point when the Load Last button is chosen, the new undertaking will be consequently repositioned to utilize the rest of the space on the paper. The Cricut Expression 2 machine will naturally choose the Load Last setting after each cut.

Apply All

The Apply All page is a simple method to apply numerous settings to the pictures in an undertaking simultaneously.

Utilizing the controls around there, you can choose settings for each picture in your present undertaking, for example, picking:

- genuine or Relative Size
- Flip Vertical
- Flip Horizontal
- Rotate

- Size
- Paper Saver
- Kerning

Paper Saver

Paper Saver naturally orchestrates the pictures in your task so it utilizes minimal measure of paper conceivable.

Kerning

This element enables you to change the dispersing between pictures. A negative worth will diminish the dividing among pictures, and a positive worth will expand the dispersing.

In the wake of choosing every one of the regions you wish to modify, press the Save button at the base right corner of the screen to roll out the improvements. You can drop any progressions you have made by pressing the Cancel button at the base left of the screen. Changes caused utilizing to apply all will abrogate any past changes made to pictures in the undertaking.

If you need to fix changes that have recently been made utilizing the Apply All page, press the fix Apply All button.

Instruments

The instruments button enables you to characterize and spare profiles for devices you work with regularly.

Each profile contains a mark for the device and a number which determines the profundity that ought to be set for the device on the sharp edge get together preceding cutting. To spare another Material profile:

1. Press the new Tool button.

2. Enter a name for the instrument.

3. Press the spare button.

If you rule against sparing the new profile, you can drop the profile creation by pressing the Cancel button rather than spare. You can erase an instrument by choosing it in the dropdown menu and pressing the Delete button. You can alter the name of a recently made custom device by pressing the Edit button, rolling out the ideal improvements, and afterward pressing the spare button.

Materials

The Materials button enables you to characterize and spare profiles for materials you work with frequently. Each profile contains data about the speed, pressure, multi-cut, and cutting device utilized while working with the material. To spare another Material profile:

1. Press the new Material button.

2. Enter a name for the material profile.

3. Press the spare button.

4. Select the ideal instrument.

5. Enter the ideal weight esteem.

6. Enter the ideal Speed esteem.

7. Enter the ideal Multi-Cut worth.

8. Press the spare button.

If you rule against sparing the new profile, you can drop the profile creation by pressing the Cancel button rather than spare. You can erase a profile by choosing it in the dropdown menu and pressing the Delete button.

Machine Settings

The Machine Settings button opens a screen which contains four settings which control the general conduct of your Cricut Expression 2 machine.

The Increments buttons enable you to choose the estimation increases. You can choose from:

- 1/4"

- 1/10"

- Centimeters

- Millimeters

The reset Machine Settings button enables you to restore the entirety of the settings on your Cricut Expression 2 machine to the plant defaults. These defaults are:

Project Quantity: 1

Picture Quantity: 1

Fit to page: off

Auto fill: off

Mat Size: 12" x 12"

Paper Size: 12" x 12"

Start Location: 0, 0

Center point: off

Fit to Length: off

Measure: Inches

Increments: 1/4"

Light: During Cutting

Material: Medium Paper

The Cutting Light dropdown enables you to browse the accompanying choices:

• Always on

• Always off

• During Cutting

The Language Selection dropdown enables you to choose whether the marks, directions, and other data showed in the Cricut Expression 2 machine in a language other than English. Extra dialects will be accessible sometime in the not too distant future.

Subsequent to rolling out any improvement to the Machine Settings, pressing the spare button will place the progressions into impact. You can drop any progressions you have made by pressing the Cancel button at the base left of the screen.

Screen Calibration

The Screen Calibration button enables you to recalibrate the touchscreen. In the wake of pressing the Screen Calibration button, press every one of the five lines of sight on the screen as they show up and the screen will be recalibrated.

About

the About area enables you to survey significant data, for example, the end-client permit understanding, guarantee data, and the product rendition of the Cricut Expression 2 machine.

CUT SETTINGS SCREEN

The Cut Settings Screen contains settings which enable you to control the cutting of your venture.

Material Selection

If you have any recently characterized materials set up for your Cricut Expression 2 machine, you can utilize this dropdown menu to choose this material and continue by stacking your mat and pressing the Cut button.

You can likewise choose one of the pre-characterized materials in the dropdown menu. If you don't wish to choose a material, you can likewise alter the weight, speed, and multi-cut qualities legitimately by choosing the relating button.

You can likewise characterize another material by pressing the new Material button.

Apparatus Selection

If you have any recently characterized apparatuses set up for your Cricut Expression 2 machine, you can utilize this dropdown menu to choose this instrument and continue by stacking your mat and pressing the Cut button. You can likewise choose one of the pre-characterized devices in the dropdown menu. The number after the name of each of the pre-characterized instruments indicates the profundity that ought to be set for that device on the edge get together before cutting.

You can likewise characterize another apparatus by pressing the new Tool button.

Cutting heavyweight or Lightweight Materials

Your Cricut Expression 2 machine can cut an assortment of materials. For an ideal cut on lightweight materials, for example, vellum or heavyweight materials, for example, slender cardstock, you may need to alter the blade profundity, speed of the cut, or cut weight.

At the point when you discover settings that function admirably for you, make certain to spare them so you can utilize them again later on.

Modifying Blade Depth

Expel the cutting sharp edge gathering from the Cricut Expression 2 machine to change the setting on the alteration handle. Nonetheless, if the bolt is looking ahead, you can leave the cutting sharp edge get together joined and basically turn the highest point of the alteration handle to change the setting.

Caution! Continuously unplug your Cricut Expression 2 machine before evacuating the blade gathering!

To evacuate the blade gathering (Figure 1), first turn the Cricut Expression 2 machine off. Find the screw and turn it counterclockwise until it relaxes enough that you can swing the screw to the privilege (Figure 2). Be mindful so as not to extricate the screw excessively, or it will drop out. Expel the blade get together from the machine. Next, find the alteration handle (Figure 3) on the highest point of the cutting sharp edge get together and go it to your ideal setting.

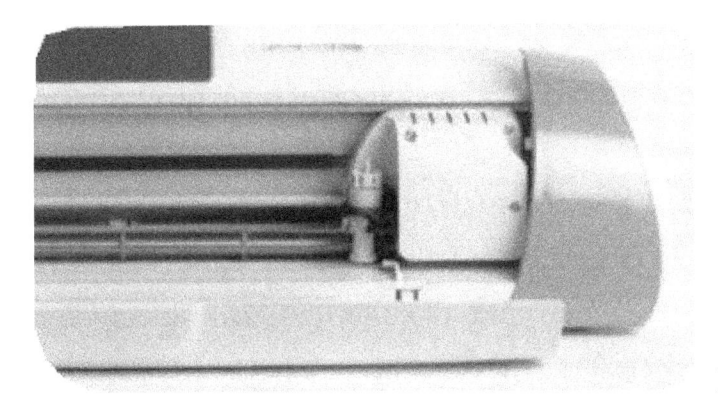

Figure.1

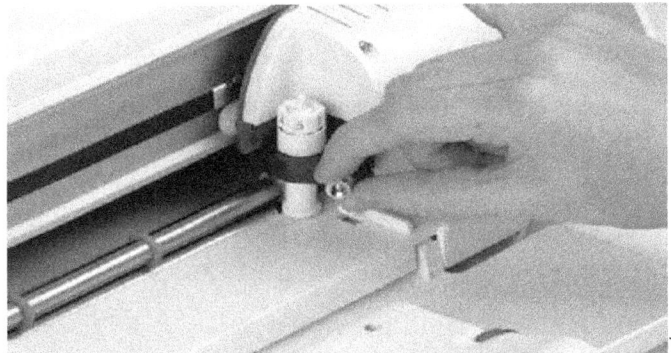

Figure.2

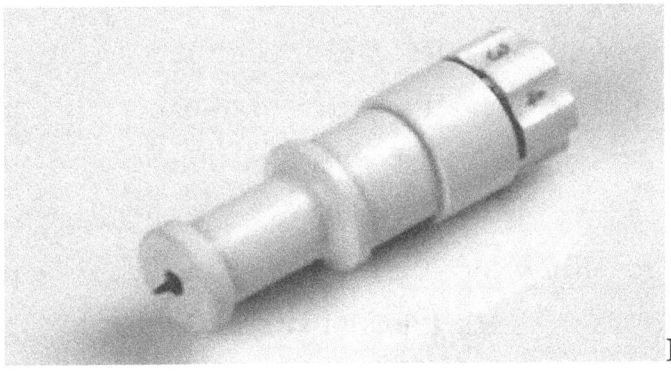

Figure.3

The littler the number on the alteration handle, the shorter the sharp edge profundity will be. Shorter edge profundities are prescribed for lightweight materials and longer edge profundities for heavier materials. Reinstall the cutting sharp edge get together into the Cricut Expression 2 machine by turning around the method to evacuate the blade get together. Test the setting on a piece bit of paper and make modifications as important.

Tip: Cutting on cardstock and other overwhelming materials will decrease the life of your edge; however it will deliver the best cuts.

Tip: If the Cricut Expression 2 machine produces poor cutting outcomes, consistently embed another sharp edge first before attempting different alternatives.

Altering Cut Speed

The Cut Speed button enables you to control the cutting velocity for an ideal cut on an assortment of papers. If you routinely cut straightforward shapes, you might need to modify this setting up to speed up. For lightweight materials or for littler, increasingly itemized cuts, you might need to turn the setting down to diminish the cutting pace. After every change, you should test the setting with a piece bit of paper, rearranging as essential until you accomplish the ideal outcomes.

The present cut speed is shown in the center area of the Cut Speed popup box. You can change the incentive by pressing the Increase and Decrease fastens and afterward pressing the spare button. When in doubt, decline the cutting velocity if your cuts are being torn. If this doesn't work, you may need to change the cut weight, modify the sharp edge profundity, or supplant the edge.

Modifying Cut pressure

The weight button enables you to control how hard the cutting instrument presses against the paper. For heavyweight materials, you might need to move the setting up to expand the cut weight. For lightweight materials, you might need to change the setting down to diminish the weight. After every alteration, you should test the setting with a piece bit of paper, correcting as important until you accomplish the ideal outcomes.

The present weight esteem is shown in the center segment of the Cut Pressure popup box. You can change the incentive by pressing the Increase and Decrease fastens and afterward pressing the spare button. When in doubt, increment the weight if your determinations are not being sliced totally through the paper. If this doesn't work, the cut speed or edge profundity may be balanced.

Multi-Cut

The Multi-Cut button enables you to slice an undertaking up to multiple times over the first cut lines. This enables the machine to cut thicker materials, for example, slight chipboard. It

Is suggested that you set your blade profundity to 6 when utilizing Multi-Cut, since the adequacy of disregarding the edge a similar cut is constrained by sharp edge profundity.

The current Multi-Cut worth is shown in the center segment of the Multi-Cut popup box. You can change the incentive by pressing the Increase and Decrease fastens and afterward pressing the spare button.

Load/unload Mat

At the point when you have finished your task and are prepared to cut, the following stage is to mount your paper on the cutting mat and press the Cut button. At the point when you arrive at the following screen, at that point:

1. Insert the mat into the machine with the bolt highlighting the machine.

2. Hold the cutting mat immovably between the roller bar and the deck beneath it and delicately drive the mat into the rollers.

3. Press the Load Mat button.

The Cricut Expression 2 machine will at that point load the paper. If it doesn't, pressing a similar button will unload the mat and enable you to begin the procedure once more. You can likewise stack the mat utilizing a similar Load/unload Mat button situated on the Home screen.

When the mat has been stacked into the Cricut Expression 2 machine, press the Cut button to start cutting your task. Pressing the interruption button will stop the cut. To start the cut once more, press the button a subsequent time. Pressing the stop button will stop the cutting and brief you by asking whether you need to launch the mat or return to the Home screen to keep structuring with the mat still stacked into the Cricut Expression 2 machine.

Fundamental Care

Blade Life

You can expect somewhere in the range of 500 to 1500 single cuts from your cutting sharp edge before it requires substitution. Your real cutting sharp edge life will fluctuate, contingent upon the settings you use and the materials you cut. At the point when the nature of your cuts diminishes, it is likely time to supplant your blade. For best outcomes, utilize just certifiable Cricut Replacement Cutting Blades, accessible at taking an interest Cricut retailers (part #290002).

Supplanting the Cutting Blade

Caution! Continuously unplug your Cricut Expression 2 machine before supplanting the cutting sharp edge.

To change the cutting sharp edge, you should initially evacuate the blade get together. to evacuate the cutting sharp edge get together (Figure 1), find the screw and turn it counterclockwise until it releases enough that you can swing the screw to one side (Figure 2). Be mindful so as not to release the screw excessively, or it will drop out.

Expel the blade get together from the machine. In the wake of expelling the cutting sharp edge get together, find the edge discharge at the highest point of the blade get together and push it in (Figure 3). The edge will rise up out of the cutting sharp edge gathering. You should tenderly force the sharp edge away from the magnet holding it set up (Figure 4).

To introduce the new edge, first expel the defensive spread from the new blade. Cautiously embed the pole of the sharp edge into the gap in the base of the blade get together. The blade ought to be sucked up inside the pole if appropriately introduced (Figure 5). The substitution blade is presently introduced. Spot the defensive spread over the old blade and discard it. Reinstall the cutting sharp edge get together into the Cricut Expression 2 machine by turning around the system to expel the blade gathering.

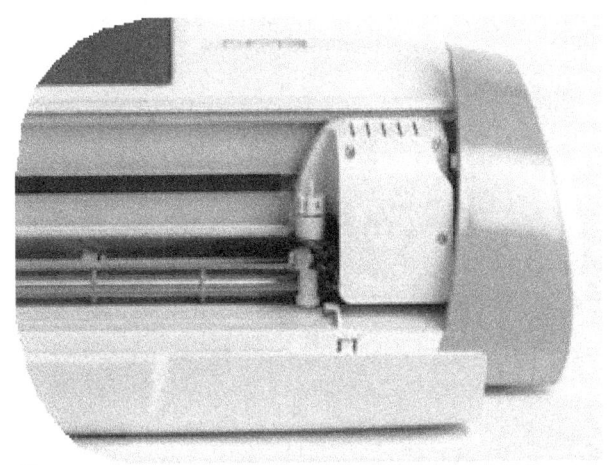

Figure.1

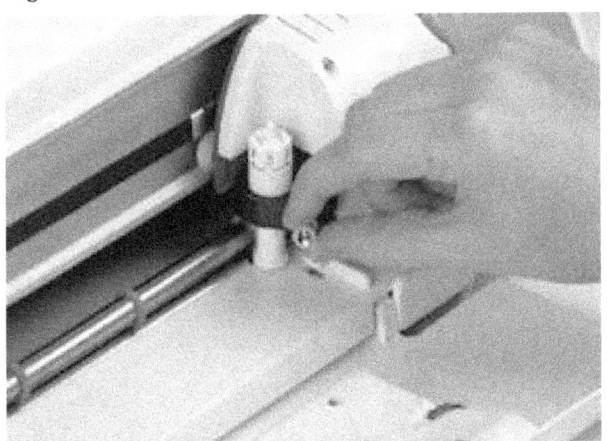

Figure.2

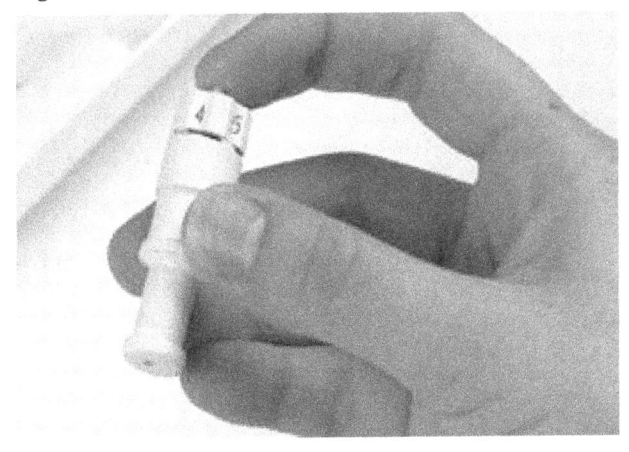

Figure.3

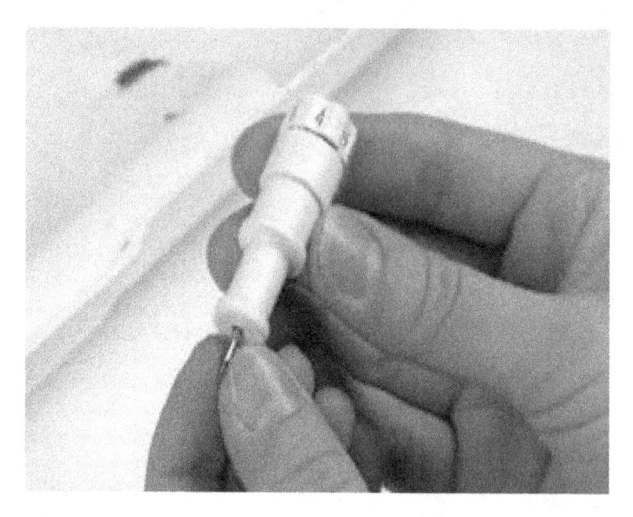

Figure.4

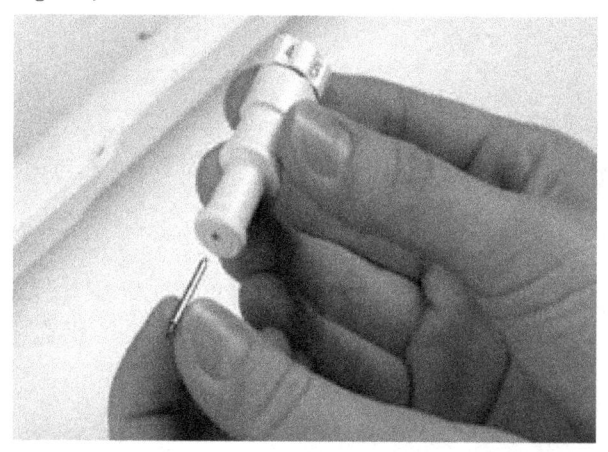

Figure 5

Caution! Blades are incredibly sharp and ought to be taken care of with the most extreme consideration. They are additionally potential stifling dangers; they ought to be avoided kids.

Caring for the Cutting Mat

You can expect somewhere in the range of 25 to 40 full mat cuts (expect considerably more when a cut is littler than the full mat) from your Cricut Expression 2 cutting mat before it requires substitution. Your genuine cutting mat life will change, contingent upon the settings you use and the papers you cut. The time has come to supplant your mat when:

• Your paper never again adheres to the cutting mat.

• The mat gets twisted on the blades

Utilize just real Cricut Expression 2 substitution cutting mats, accessible at retailers all over.

Cleaning your Cricut Expression 2 Machine

Caution! Continuously unplug your Cricut Expression 2 machine before cleaning!

To clean the Cricut Expression 2 machine, tenderly wipe outside boards with a clammy material. Promptly dry any abundance dampness with a chamois or other delicate fabric. Try not to utilize synthetic compounds or liquor based cleaners (counting, yet not restricted to, $CH_3)_2CO$, benzene, and carbon tetrachloride) on the machine. Rough chemicals and cleaning apparatuses ought to likewise be stayed away from. Try not to drench the machine or any part of it in water.

Extra Basic Care Tips

• Keep away from nourishment and fluids.

- Keep in dry, sans dust area.
- Avoid extreme warmth or cold.
- Do not leave in vehicle, where extreme warmth may dissolve or harm plastic parts.
- Do not open to coordinate daylight for any all-inclusive timeframe.

Discretionary Adapter Installation

Your Cricut Expression 2 machine has a connector opening in the back to empower future usefulness, for example, Wi-Fi. If it's not too much trouble see documentation included with future connectors for establishment guidelines.

TROUBLESHOOTING

Issue: the cutting mat didn't stack when I pressed the Load button.

Solution: Press the unload Mat fasten and afterward reload the mat before pressing the Cut button once more.

Issue: the sharp edge isn't carving completely through the paper.

Solution 1: Adjust the Multi-Cut setting on the slice screen to consider various cuts along similar cutting lines.

Solution 2: Increase the cut weight in the Project Preview screen.

Solution 3: the sharp edge profundity should be balanced, especially if you are attempting to slice through thicker materials.

Solution 4: the blade may have gotten dull and should be supplanted.

Issue: the paper lifts off the mat as the Cricut Expression 2 machine is cutting.

Solution 1: Make sure you press the paper solidly onto the cutting mat when setting up the cut.

Solution 2: Rinse the mat with water while tenderly focusing on the paper building up on the mat. Let the mat completely dry before endeavoring to re-utilize the mat.

Solution 3: take a stab at utilizing another mat. Each mat will last somewhere in the range of 25 to 40 full page cuts, contingent upon the size of cuts and the sort of material you are cutting.

Issue: the cutting mat is excessively clingy. It's tearing my paper when I attempt to expel it. **Solution:** Use a specialty blade or the Cricut devices (sold independently) to effectively lift the material from the cutting mat. The Cricut instruments are specially crafted for lifting, pulling, or tidying up cut characters.

Issue: My machine doesn't turn on and doesn't seem, by all accounts, to be getting any force.

Solution 1: Check the force connector to ensure that the green force marker is lit up. If it isn't lit, check to ensure the force plug is totally embedded into the force connector.

Solution 2: attempt to plug the force rope into another outlet.

Issue: My Cricut Expression 2 machine doesn't impart to a connected USB gadget.

Solution 1: Check the USB link to ensure that it is appropriately associated.

Solution 2: Make sure that the associated gadget is controlled on.

Solution 3: Make sure that the Cricut Expression 2 machine and the joined gadget have the most recent firmware introduced.

CRICUTEXPRESSION 2 MACHINE STATEMENT OF LIMITED WARRANTY

Section 1—General Terms

This Statement of Limited Warranty incorporates Part 1—General terms, Part 2—Country-Specific terms, and Part 3—Warranty Information. The conditions of Part 2 supplant or adjust those of Part 1. The guarantees gave by Provocraft

And Novelty, INC. ("Provocraft") or its approved fix focus in this Statement of Limited Warranty apply just to Machines you buy for your utilization and not for resale. The expression "Machine" signifies a Cricut Expression 2 machine, its highlights, components, or adornments, including any textual style or picture cartridges sold therewith, or any blend of them. The expression "Machine" does exclude any extra or buyer replaceable parts, including yet not constrained to cutting sharp blades and cutting mats. Nothing in this Statement of Limited Warranty influences any statutory privileges of purchasers that can't be deferred or constrained by contract.

What this Warranty Covers

Provocraft warrants that each Machine 1) is liberated from abandons in materials and workmanship and 2) will perform generously as portrayed in the going with User Manual. The guarantee time frame for the Machine begins the first Date of Purchase and is indicated in Part 3— Warranty Information. The date on your receipt or deals receipt is the Date of Purchase except if Provocraft or your affiliate illuminates you generally. A section that replaces an expelled part will expect the guarantee administration status of the evacuated part. Except if Provocraft indicates something else, these guarantees apply just in the nation or district in which you bought the Machine.

These warranties are your exclusive warranties and replace all other warranties or conditions, express or implied, including, but not limited to, the implied warranties or conditions of merchantability and fitness for a particular purpose.

A few states or jurisdictions do not allow the exclusion of express or implied warranties, so the above exclusion may not apply to you. In that event, such warranties are limited in duration to the warranty period. No warranties apply after that period. A few states or jurisdictions do not allow limitations on how long an implied warranty endures, so the above limitation may not apply to you.

What this Warranty Does not Cover

This guarantee doesn't cover the accompanying:

1. Blade lodging and cutting sharp blades, regardless of whether provided with the Machine or sold independently from the Machine;

2. Cutting mats, regardless of whether provided with the Machine or sold independently from the Machine;

3. Failure coming about because of abuse (counting yet not constrained to use past the Machine's ability or capacity), use in a business or for business purposes, mishap, change, unacceptable physical or working condition, or ill-advised upkeep by you; and

4. Failure brought about by an item or utilization of outsider programming for which Provocraft isn't dependable.

The guarantee is voided by expulsion or change of distinguishing proof marks on the Machine or its parts or dismantling of any segment of the Machine. Provocraft doesn't warrant continuous or mistake free activity of a Machine.

Any specialized or other help accommodated a Machine under guarantee, for example, help with "how-to" questions and those in regards to Machine set-up and establishment, is given without warranties of any kind.

The most effective method to Obtain Warranty Service

If the Machine doesn't work as justified during the guarantee time frame, contact Cricut Customer Care at the accompanying site: www.cricut.com/guarantee.

What Provocraft Will Do to Correct Issues?

At the point when you contact client assistance, you should follow the issue assurance and goals strategies that Provocraft indicates. An underlying determination of your concern can be made either by an expert via phone or electronically by access to www.cricut.com. The kind of guarantee administration pertinent to your Machine is indicated in Part 3—Warranty Information.

You are liable for adhering to the directions that Provocraft gives.

If your concern can be settled with a Customer Replaceable Unit ("CRU"), Provocraft will deliver the CRU to you for you to introduce.

If the Machine doesn't work as justified during the guarantee time frame and your concern can't be settled via phone or electronically, or with a CRU, Provocraft will either, at its carefulness, 1) fix it to make it work as justified, or 2) supplant it with one that is in any event practically equal.

If cricut client care considers it important to restore the Machine to Provocraft for guarantee administration, client assistance will give a Return Material Authorization (RMA). After getting a RMA from client assistance, you should transport the Machine with a duplicate of your verification of procurement, and a letter containing the RMA, your name, return shipping address, and a short composed portrayal of the issue to the Provocraft Authorized Care Center.

The RMA number must show up outwardly of the transportation box. Just Machines bearing a substantial RMA will be acknowledged by Provocraft. Except if Provocraft coordinates else, we suggest you guarantee the shipment at the buy cost of the Machine. The expenses of such guaranteeing/shipping are your duty. Provocraft, at its sole prudence, will either fix or supplant your Machine, and return it shipping paid ahead of time to the location you give in the letter remembered for your arrival.

If you have any inquiries with respect to these guarantees, if it's not too much trouble reach us: www.cricut.com/guarantee.

Trade of a Machine or part

At the point when the guarantee administration includes the trading of a Machine or part, the thing Provocraft replaces turns into its property and the substitution turns into yours. You speak that every single expelled thing is real and unaltered. The substitution may not be new, however will be in acceptable working request and at any rate practically identical to the thing supplanted. The substitution accepts the guarantee administration status of the supplanted thing.

Your additional duties

Before Provocraft trades a Machine or part, you consent to expel all highlights, parts, choices, changes, and connections not under guarantee administration.

You likewise consent to:

1. Ensure that the Machine is liberated from any lawful commitments or limitations that forestall its trade; and

2. The measure of some other real direct harms up to yet not surpassing the sum paid for the Machine that is subject of the case. This cutoff likewise applies to Provocraft's providers and your affiliate. It is the most extreme for which Provocraft, its providers, and your affiliate are aggregately capable.

By no means is Provocraft, or its suppliers or resellers liable for any of the following even if informed of their possibility:
1) Third party claims against you for damages (other than those under the first it enlisted above);
2) Special, incidental, or indirect damages or for any economic consequential damages;
3) Loss for damage to any materials used in the machine or
4) lost profits, business revenue, altruism, or anticipated savings. A few states or jurisdictions do not allow the exclusion or limitation of incidental or consequential damages, so the above limitation or exclusion may not apply to you. A few states or jurisdictions do not allow limitations on how long an implied warranty lasts, so the above limitation may not apply to you.

Limitation of Liability

Both you and Provocraft agree to the utilization of the laws of the nation wherein you procured the Machine to oversee, decipher, and implement the entirety of your and Provocraft's privileges, obligations, and commitments emerging from, or relating in any way to, the topic of this Statement of Limited Warranty, regardless of contention of law standards.

These warranties give you specific legal rights and you may also have other rights which vary from state to state or jurisdiction to jurisdiction.

Jurisdiction

The entirety of our privileges, obligations, and commitments are dependent upon the courts of the nation in which you obtained the Machine.

Section 2—Country-Specific Terms

CANADA

Restriction of Liability: the accompanying replaces thing 1 of this segment:

1. harms for substantial damage (counting passing) or physical mischief to genuine property and unmistakable individual property brought about by Provocraft's carelessness; and Governing Law: the accompanying replaces "laws of the nation in which you obtained the Machine" in the main sentence: laws in the Province of Ontario.

US

Governing Law: the accompanying replaces "laws of the nation in which you gained the Machine" in the primary sentence: laws of the State of Utah.

Jurisdiction: the accompanying replaces "nation in which you procured the Machine" in the main sentence: State of Utah.

Section 3—Warranty Information

This Part 3 gives data in regards to the guarantee relevant to your Machine, including the guarantee time frame and sort of guarantee administration Provocraft gives.

Guarantee period

The guarantee time frame may differ by nation or area.

A guarantee time of 1 year on electronic parts including engines, wiring, switches, speed controls, LCD screens, and other electronic segments; and 90 days work. A guarantee time of 90 days on all non-electronic segments. If a disappointment of a non-electronic part happens inside 90 days of the first buy date, Provocraft will fix or supplant the segment. You will be liable for restoring the segment to Provocraft for guarantee administration (allude to page 2 for guidelines about delivery to Provocraft).

A guarantee time of 90 days on all Cricut marked picture or textual style cartridges.

Sorts of Warranty administration

Whenever required, Provocraft gives fix or trade administration relying upon the sort of guarantee administration determined for your Machine as depicted beneath. Booking of administration will rely on the hour of your call and is liable to parts accessibility. Administration levels are reaction time targets and are not ensured. The predetermined degree of guarantee administration may not be accessible in every single overall area. Extra charges may apply outside Provocraft's typical assistance territory. Contact your neighborhood Provocraft agent or your affiliate for nation and area explicit data.

1. Customer Replaceable Unit ("CRU") Service

At the point when material, Provocraft will give a swap CRU to you for you to introduce.

CRU data and supplanting directions are dispatched with any CRU. Establishment of a CRU is your obligation. If Provocraft introduces a CRU at your solicitation, you will be charged for the establishment. At the point when return is required, 1) return guidelines and a holder are sent with the substitution CRU, and 2) you might be charged for the substitution CRU if Provocraft doesn't get the flawed CRU inside 30 days of your receipt of the substitution.

2. Courier or Depot Service

At the point when relevant, Provocraft will furnish you with a transportation holder for you to restore your Machine to an assigned help focus. A messenger will get your Machine and convey it to the assigned assistance focus. Following its fix or trade, Provocraft will orchestrate the arrival conveyance of the Machine to your area. You are answerable for its establishment and confirmation.

3. Customer Carry-In or Mail-In Service When appropriate, you will convey or mail as Provocraft indicates (paid ahead of time except if Provocraft determines something else) the bombing Machine reasonably bundled to an area Provocraft assigns. After Provocraft has fixed or traded the Machine, Provocraft will make it accessible for your assortment or, for Mail-in Service, Provocraft will return it to you at Provocraft's cost, except if Provocraft indicates something else.

Chapter Three: Setting a New Cricut Machine Up Using Software

(Load And Unload Paper)

1. DEFINITIONS. "Software" signifies any machine intelligible materials (counting, yet not restricted to, source code, accumulated code, calculations, libraries, source documents, header records, also, information documents), any updates or blunder revisions gave by PROVO CRAFT, and any client or proprietor manuals, programming guides, and other documentation gave to you by PROVO CRAFT under this AGREEMENT. "Firmware" signifies any encoded data gave on any chip or microchip of CRICUT EXPRESSION including, however not constrained to, source code, ordered code, calculations, libraries, source records, header records, and information documents, and any updates or mistake revisions gave by PROVO CRAFT.

"Hardware" signifies any physical segment that is a piece of or sold with CRICUT EXPRESSION, including yet not constrained to Cricut™ cartridges utilized with

CRICUT EXPRESSION that contain pictures or textual styles. "Documentation" signifies any reports gave CRICUT EXPRESSION when acquired, including however not constrained to the User Manual.

2. Permit TO USE. Subject to the terms and states of this AGREEMENT, PROVO Art awards you a non-select, non-transferable, constrained permit without permit charges to utilize CRICUT EXPRESSION and any related programming, firmware, and equipment.

3. Limitations. Programming and firmware are classified and copyrighted. Title to programming, firmware, and equipment and all related protected innovation rights is held by PROVO CRAFT. Except if implementation is precluded by appropriate law, you may not change, decompile, dismantle, figure out, circulate, or duplicate programming, firmware, or equipment. You may not, regardless of whether for your very own utilization or advantage or for the utilization or advantage of another, aside from as explicitly gave in this, duplicate, duplicate, or distribute, or grant the generation, duplicating, or production of, any physical, mechanical, electrical, or electronic medium that is related with the CRICUT EXPRESSION, counting any firmware, programming, and documentation, aside from as explicitly gave in this. No right, title, or enthusiasm for or to any trademark, administration imprint, logo, or exchange name of PROVO CRAFT or its licensors is allowed under this AGREEMENT.

4. Move. You may forever move the entirety of your privileges under this AGREEMENT as it were as a feature of a deal or move of the CRICUT EXPRESSION, if you hold no duplicates of any part or segment of the CRICUT EXPRESSION, you move the entirety of the CRICUT Articulation (counting all segment parts, equipment, programming and updates thereof, furthermore, documentation), and the beneficiary consents to the details of this AGREEMENT.

If you have purchased a new Cricut machine and now you don't know where to start...Well, we as a whole have been there, so don't stress it isn't as intricate as it first looks.

For your new Cricut, you will likewise need to have an online record so you can utilize Cricut's Design Studio which is the working programming for Cricut machines. The product bolsters just more current machines which are Explore, Explore One, Explore Air 1 and 2 and new Cricut creator machine.

Did you realize you don't generally require a machine to have a record in DS? Truly, you are going to require the machine to remove things, yet you don't really must have it to mess with the pictures and programming.

So on the off chance that you have quite recently purchased another machine, it might be a good thought to jump into the DS with the goal that when your Cricut land at your front entryway you will realize a little better about what to do straightaway.

Similarly as some other ability, Cricut creating likewise have a learning way and figuring out how to utilize DS before you have the machine may make it somewhat simpler.

To make a record, go to www.cricut.com/arrangement and snap on the green begin button. Next, a screen with a module download shows up. Snap Download. When downloaded, open or show it to double tapping on it. (If you can't discover it, it ought to be in your download organizer on your PC). Cricut installer will show up, click straightaway, read and acknowledge the understanding and afterward click Install button. At the point when the establishment is finished, click done in installer window and afterward proceed with button in the program. You will be diverted to a Cricut sign in screen. In the event that you as of now have Cricut ID account, at that point simply sign in. In the event that this is your first time, you should join first.

You just need one ID represent your Cricut. Regardless of whether you have numerous machines, they all can be gone through one record. In the event that you buy computerized picture through Cricut site, the picture will be transferred to the record you bought it under and can't be utilized it in different records.

To make Cricut ID account click make Cricut ID button, fill in required subtleties and acknowledge the terms of utilization.

Ensure your subtleties are right in such a case that you ever purchase physical merchandise from the Cricut site; they will require a right conveyance address.

A portion of the recently acquired machines accompany a free preliminary. The preliminary will begin when you initially interface the machine to the PC.

To effectively open the plan space you can simply go to www.cricut.com and click the structure in the highest point of the site or essentially click the Cricut application symbol which ought to have been introduced on your PC after the Cricut application establishment process.

You will worship your Cricut machine once you find a good pace more. DS is an essentially designated realistic program so in the event that you stall out, don't get baffled. To get familiar with all in DS will take some time, yet once you ace it, it sure will be justified, despite all the trouble.

Chapter Three: Maintenance of The Cricut Machine

How would I clean my Explore machine?

After some time, and with use, your machine may gather residue or paper particles, or you may see a portion of the oils from the machine start to expand upon the carriage track. Cleaning it is simple!

Consider the accompanying tips when cleaning your Explore machine:

- Continuously separate the machine from power before cleaning it.
- The machine itself can be cleaned utilizing glass cleaner splashed on a delicate clean fabric.
- If you watch friction based electricity develop causing residue or paper particles to amass, you can just wipe that away with a clean delicate material.

- If you see a development of oil on the bar across which the carriage ventures, you can utilize a cotton swab, tissue, or a delicate material and tenderly expel it.

Significant: *Never utilize any sort of CH3)2CO, for example, nail clean remover, as that will for all time harm the plastic surfaces of the machine.*

Grease Application Instructions

- Turn off the Cricut Explore machine.
- Move the Cut Smart carriage by pushing it gradually to one side.
- Clean the Cut Smart carriage bar with a tissue, cleaning around the whole bar (the carriage bar is the one the Cut Smart carriage slides on, just before the belt).
- Move the Cut Smart carriage by pushing it gradually to one side.
- Repeat the way toward cleaning the Cut Smart carriage bar with a tissue, cleaning around the whole bar.
- Gradually move the Cut Smart carriage to the focal point of the machine.
- Open the oil parcel and press a modest quantity of oil onto the finish of the cotton swab.
- On the two sides of the Cut Smart carriage, apply a light covering of oil around the bar to shape a ¼" ring on each side of the carriage.

- Gradually move the Cut Smart carriage right to one side and afterward right to one side to appropriate the oil equally along the whole bar.
- Wipe off any oil development at the parts of the bargains.

Significant: *Keep out of the span of youngsters. This item may aggravate the skin or eyes. In case of contact with skin or eyes, quickly wash altogether with water and look for restorative consideration if vital. Wash hands altogether in the wake of dealing with.*

Cleaning the Cutting Blade

THE CRICUT BLADES: WHAT'S THE BIG DIFFERENCE?

On the off chance that you don't utilize the correct sharp edge for your Cricut, it might cutting TOO DEEP. So check your bundling and be cautious when purchasing substitution Cricut blades.

PREMIUM POINT BLADE (FITS IN EXPLORE AND MAKER):

The Deep-Point Blade is an extraordinary sharp edge that cuts further than the standard fine point blade. This blade has a more extreme sharp edge (60 degrees versus 45 degrees for the other fine point blades) and harder, progressively solid steel.

I've utilized it for THICKER tasks on my Cricut Explore and Maker. On the off chance that you locate your fine point sharp edge simply wouldn't like to slice through a material thicker than standard cardstock, this is the blade to utilize. You can distinguish a profound point blade outside of its bundling by the shade of its top, which is BLUE or BLACK/BROWN. Here is the Deep-Point Blade cutting cowhide:

Bonded FABRIC BLADE (FITS IN EXPLORE AND MAKER):

On the off chance that you like to cut texture on your Explore, the Bonded Fabric Blade is the edge for you. This edge will remain more keen longer when cutting texture. While it fits both the Explore and Maker, it's truly proposed for the Explore as the Maker has other sharp edge alternatives for texture, similar to the rotating blade.

Rotational BLADE (FITS IN MAKER ONLY):

Texture cutters will need to utilize the Rotary Blade in their Maker. This blade has a modest rotational wheel that can cut incredibly complicated structures. You can likewise utilize this sharp edge for crepe paper with incredible achievement! Essentially, the rotating edge is extraordinary for any material that would catch on a customary sharp edge.

KNIFE BLADE (FITS IN MAKER ONLY):

Got something extremely thick to cut? The Knife Blade is your answer! This resembles a scaled down and extremely sharp Xacto blade and it can truly get in there to cut the intense stuff. I've utilized my blade to cut wood and calfskin.

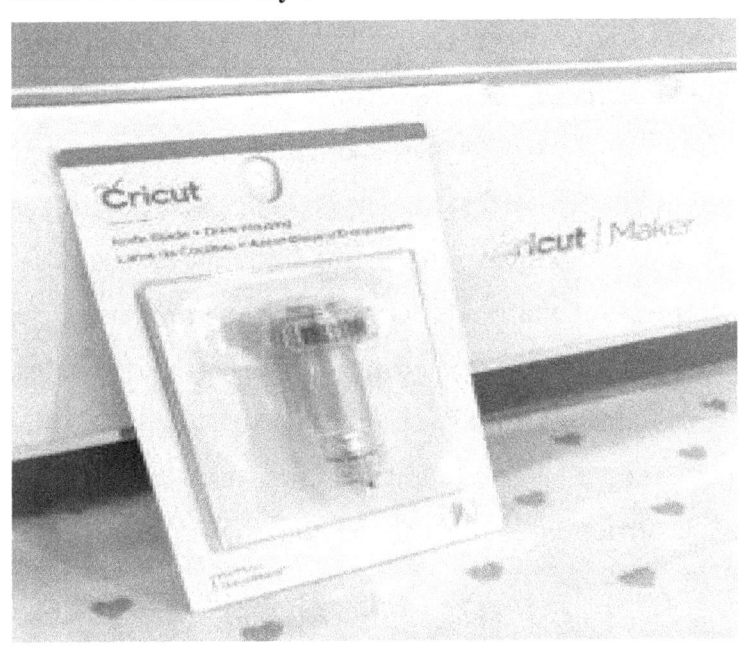

SCORING WHEEL and DOUBLE SCORING WHEEL (FITS IN MAKER ONLY):

The scoring wheels don't really cut — rather, they score. The Cricut Scoring Wheel resembles the rotating sharp edge; however it won't really slice through your material.

It accompanies two hints: the single scoring tip and the twofold scoring tip.

Utilize the single scoring tip for light materials like cardstock. Utilize the twofold scoring tip for harder to overlap materials like cardboard.

ENGRAVING TIP (FITS IN MAKER ONLY)

The etching Tip is another Cricut Maker Tool that lets you imprint metal, acrylic, cowhide, and paper. The etching apparatus lets you etch on level, delicate metals, (for example, aluminum and copper), calfskin, acrylic, and paper. With the etching tip, you can imprint interesting and changeless plans on an assortment of materials for a wide range of tasks, for example, complicatedly engraved pooch labels, name plates, recorded workmanship, home stylistic theme, gems, exquisite monograms, and treasure quality mementos. The etching device is $44.99 for both the tip and lodging, or $24.99 for simply the tip.

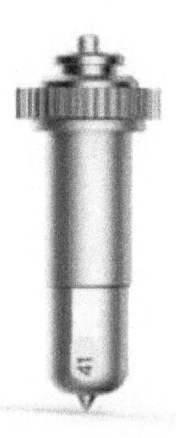

FINE DEBOSSING TIP (FITS IN MAKER ONLY)

Fine Debossing Tip is another Cricut Maker Tool that lets you deboss cowhide and paper. The debossing apparatus pushes the material IN to make pretty impacts — it's something contrary to an embellishing device. Deboss any plan you'd like, including brightening thrives, designs, monograms, logos, seals, and the sky is the limit from there.

This moving debossing ball, with a more extensive scope of movement, gives you free rule to alter, customize, and plan with fantastic multifaceted nature. Make a dimensional wedding card, note to say thanks with your monogram, or add thrive to blessing boxes, labels, and then some. Makes a shocking impact on foil cardstock, covered paper, sparkle and sparkle paper, foil cardstock, basswood, and considerably more. The debossing instrument is $44.99 for both the tip and lodging, or $24.99 for simply the tip.

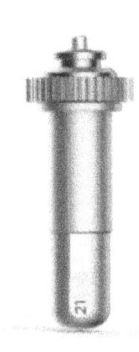

PERFORATION BLADE (FITS IN MAKER ONLY)

The puncturing blades another Cricut Maker Tool that lets you puncture materials like paper. The aperture instrument makes simple holes for tear-offs and simple strip always utilizing paper, cardstock, acetic acid derivation, blurb board, and the sky is the limit from there! Get the ideal tear rapidly and easily with exact aperture cuts for a wide assortment of activities. To make uniform, finely punctured lines for any plan, simply snap this tip onto the QuickSwap Housing and advise your Cricut Maker to "Go!" Evenly dispersed aperture lines take into account spotless, in any event, tearing without the need to overlap heretofore – particularly incredible for shapes with bends. Ideal for detach booklet pages, pool tickets, custom made diaries, or for any venture that requests a perfect tear. For use with Cricut Maker machines. This is an essential Perforation Blade with 2.5 mm teeth/0.5 mm holes. The puncturing device is $44.99 for both the sharp edge tip and lodging, or $24.99 for simply the tip.

EDGING BLADE (FITS IN MAKER ONLY)

The wavy edge is another Cricut Maker Tool that lets you edge materials like paper. This device will make a wavy edge instead of a straight edge to give you an embellishing edge quicker. This is an exceptional etched hardened steel blade that lets you make unique vinyl decals, iron-on plans, envelopes, cards, blessing labels, and composition ventures, or whenever you need impressively completed blades and in vogue configuration emphasizes. Ideal for iron-on, vinyl, paper, cardstock, texture, and that's only the tip of the iceberg. For use with Cricut Maker machines. The wavy blade is 2.0 mm L/0.8 mm H. The wavy edging edge is $44.99 for both the edge tip and lodging, or $24.99 for simply the tip.

INSTALLING A NEW CRICUT BLADE

To begin with, it's imperative to comprehend that Cricut sharp blades truly come in two sections — the blade itself and the edge lodging. You need BOTH to introduce and cut with them on your Cricut. All new Cricuts accompany a Fine Point Blade and Blade Housing, yet on the off chance that you go to the store to get a substitution blade, you just need the substitution sharp edge, not a totally different edge lodging (except if you lost yours or something to that effect).

This is what another Deep-Point substitution blade looks like without anyone by itself:

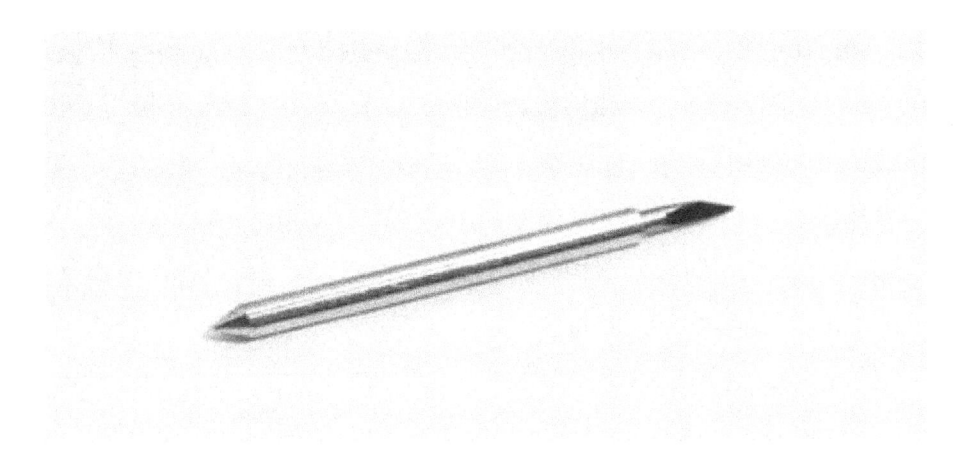

At the point when you feel it's an ideal opportunity to get another fine point or profound point sharp edge and introduce it in your lodging, this is what you do:

1. Purchase a Premium Fine-Point Blade (for a fine point blade lodging) or a Deep-Point Blade (for a profound point sharp edge lodging). Note that these two sharp blades have various lodgings — they are not exchangeable.

2. Open the clasp and evacuate the blade lodging.

3. Push the plunger on the highest point of the sharp edge lodging and delicately pull out the blade from the base. Be cautious—it's sharp! Put it in a safe spot.

4. Expel the little plastic spread from the new blade.

5. Put the pole of the new blade into the sharp edge lodging. There's a magnet in the sharp edge lodging that will hold the new blade set up.

6. Supplant the blade lodging in the machine. (See Changing Your Cricut Blade Housings underneath).

7. Put the little plastic spread you expelled from the new blade onto the tip of your old sharp edge to prevent it from harming you or any other person.

Shouldn't something be said about introducing another rotary blade for the Cricut Maker? This is what you do when you're prepared to transform it:

1. Purchase a Rotary Blade Kit.
2. Expel the rotary blade lodging from your Maker.
3. Open your Rotary Blade Kit, evacuate the defensive plastic spread, and slip it over your current turning edge with the huge opening over the lodging screw. Ensure you feel the defensive spread fit properly.
4. Utilize the screw driver gave in your pack to expel the screw from the lodging. Keep the sharp blade inside the defensive spread as you do this.
5. Evacuate the new rotary blade, strategically located in another defensive spread, from the Rotary Blade Kit bundle.
6. Spot the new revolving blade over your lodging.
7. Supplant the screw with the screwdriver — be mindful so as not to over fix it.
8. Evacuate defensive plastic covering cautiously (recollect, that rotational blade is still sharp) and supplant the revolving edge in your Cricut (see Changing Your Cricut Blade Housings beneath).
9. Put the old blade (with the defensive spread still on it) once again into the bundling before you store or dispose of it.

CHANGING YOUR CRICUT BLADE HOUSING

Something I love about the Cricut is that it is so natural to utilize. That introducing and changing sharp blades is no special case to this!

To change the Fine Point and Deep Point Blades, you just open the clasp (clip B on the off chance that you have two braces), pull up and evacuate the blade lodging as of now in your machine, drop in another sharp edge lodging, and close the cinch. Voila!

To change the Knife Blade, Rotary Blade, or Scoring Wheel on the Cricut Maker, you simply need to ensure the rigging on the sharp edge lodging is looking toward (and fitting into) the apparatus on the Cricut. Open brace B, evacuate whatever blade lodging is there, position the new edge lodging so it fits in the rigging, and close the clip.

KEEPING YOUR CRICUT BLADES SHARP

Utilizing a similar Premium Fine-Point Blade for over a year now is actual, and there's a stunt to it! Instead of supplanting my edge each time it is by all accounts getting dull and not cutting like it should, I am ready to fix it. There's two different ways I do this:

1. Ball up a sheet of aluminum foil, expel the blade lodging from the Cricut, discourage the plunger, and stick the sharp edge into the aluminum foil ball again and again. I do jab the point in around multiple times. This assists with evacuating any bits of paper or vinyl that may be adhered to the blade and furthermore appears to hone it. This method works for the Fine-Point and Deep-Point Blades.

THE MAGIC OF THE ALUMINUM FOIL BALL!

BEFORE **AFTER**

2. Spread a bit of aluminum foil on your cutting mat and cut a straightforward plan in it. It will help hone your sharp edge a piece and doesn't necessitate that you expel your lodging. This strategy works for all blades.

Another approach to keep your blades more honed is to utilize an alternate blade to cut paper than the edge you use to cut vinyl—it will broaden the life of the edge and make for more honed cuts. Shading code your blades by painting the tip of the plastic sharp edge spread with some acrylic paint—white for paper, dark for vinyl, and so forth.

Step by step instructions to Clean Your Cricut Cutting Mat

Here, we will cover how to clean and keep up your cutting mats whether you're utilizing a Cricut mat or a Silhouette.

We as a whole expertise knows how baffling it can be when starting a new project and your material won't adhere to the outside of your cutting mat.

The inquiries most occasions are tied in with is cleaning and restocking cutting mats, particularly after they've been utilized to cut felt.

Here are explanations on how you can dispose of the entire developed gunk.

We'll go over resticking your cutting mat when it's never again working and end with certain tips and replies to your habitually posed inquiries.

We should get sticky... I mean... began!

Instructions to Clean Your Mat (Method 1: Gentle Cycle)

At the point when you find that your Cricut mat is never again clingy enough to appropriately hold your materials, attempt these strategies to clean your mat and inhale some life over into it.

As your mat gathers grime and flotsam and jetsam with your caring use, descend the rundown to increasingly strong cleaning strategies.

Be delicate with your mats, and they may even last you through numerous rounds of occasion parties.

Three Cricut cutting mats: blue, green, and purple

Sticky lint roller

- Run a clingy build up roller (or circle of veiling tape) over your Cricut mat to evacuate dust, strands, bits of paper, and hairs.
- This should be possible consistently, between ventures, when you neglect to cover your Cricut mats medium-term, or just at whatever point you notice bits and filaments aggregating on your mat.
- It's an extraordinary method to expel any outstanding fragments or bits of paper, rather than attempting to follow them all with tweezers. At the point when the buildup roller or veiling tape is stickier than the mat, it

pulls all the culpable hairs and bits of paper directly off the mat! It works particularly well on the less-crude cutting mats.

- Alright for the pink Cricut Fabric Grip mats!

Infant wipes

- Delicately wipe down with unscented, liquor free, dye free infant wipes. Cream free, without cornstarch. You need indisputably the plainest wipes you can discover, so you aren't covering your cutting mats with extra creams, oils or solvents that could meddle with the tenacity or separate the adhesive.

- Let dry before utilizing.

Soap and warm water

- Wash with cleanser and warm water.
- Dish cleanser is the best to utilize, and again you need to utilize cleanser that is liberated from moisturizers that could gunk up your mat.
- Delicately scour with a fabric, delicate brush, delicate wipe, or enchantment eraser, and flush well.
- Let dry totally before utilizing.

Cautioning: *Do not utilize boiling water, as warmth has been known to twist Cricut mats, making it so they won't fit well in your machine.*

The Results

Regularly enough, basically washing your mat will be sufficient to revive its unique clingy magnificence! After your cutting mat has totally dried, try out its tenacity with a piece of the material you'll be utilizing for your next task, or a perfect finger.

If your mat has endured enough periods of undertakings, or been washed and scoured one such a large number of times, you'll have to go to something somewhat more grounded...

Instructions to Clean Your Mat (Method 2: Heavy Duty)

If those delicate cleaning techniques don't reestablish your cutting mat's usefulness, you can give or try breaking out the big guns and utilize adhesive remover to completely clean your mat.

Note: *The cleaning techniques found on this page are not for the pink Cricut Fabric Grip mat. They are for the blue, green, and purple Cricut mats. Try not to put anything wet (counting water) on your pink texture mats. you'll have to go to something somewhat more grounded...*

What is adhesive remover?

Adhesive removers are solid solvents that will disintegrate a portion of the adhesive (the clingy stick) on your mat, helping you expel the entire gunk that is adhered to it.

Cautioning: *This procedure will strip your cutting mat of adhesive, so you may need to reapply adhesive to restick your mat. Try not to stress; I'll walk you through it.*

Which adhesive would it be a good idea for you to utilize?

I prescribe utilizing Goo Gone as it has been over and again and dependably utilized by the Cricut and creating network. In any case, you don't have to purchase a totally different item for this! On the off chance that you have any kind of adhesive lying around that you're alright with, it will probably work fine and dandy.

Different choices are:
- 70% Isopropyl (scouring) liquor
- De-Solv-it Universal Stain Remover and Pre-Wash

- LA's Totally Awesome All Purpose Concentrated Cleaner

Step by step instructions to utilize adhesive to clean your Cricut mat

- Read the headings of your adhesive remover, and adjust as fundamental.
- Pour or shower a limited quantity onto your mat.
- Spread it around with a scrubber, or any solid bit of plastic like an old charge card.
- Allow the dissolvable to sit and do something amazing. The more you let the adhesive sit, the more stuff it will expel. The specific term will rely upon which dissolvable you use, so read the headings on your jug. In the event that this is your first time, I prescribe just it sit for a couple of moments to evacuate the filthy surface layer of cement. (If you have as of now reattached your mat a lot of times and are prepared for a new start, you can let it sit for up to 20-30 minutes.)
- Utilize your scrubber to scratch the filthy adhesive off your mat. You can likewise clear it off with a material or paper towels.
- Wash with soap and warm water to evacuate any extra residue.
- Let the mat dry totally

Step by step instructions to Reattach Your Cutting Mat

Alright, so by what method can we really make a Cricut mat clingy again since you realize how to clean it? Basic: simply include another layer of paste!

The ideal way

One of the best methods to reattach a slicing mat is to utilize the Zig 2-Way Glue Pen (with the Jumbo tip). This is, by a long shot, the most effortless technique for reattaching your mat. The paste comes in pen structure, so it's inconceivably simple to apply.

There's no compelling reason to tape the edges of your mat, as with cement splashes, since you can control precisely where the paste goes. Additionally, the paste goes on blue and turns clear as it dries, which makes it overly simple to ensure that you have applied an even layer to your whole cutting mat.

At the point when you first open up the pen, you may need to prime it, to ensure that the paste is coursing through the wipe at the tip. You do this by squeezing or touching the tip of the paste pen against a piece surface, until you can see the tip diverts blue from the paste.

Follow these means to reattach your cutting mat:

1. Apply the paste to the internal, gridded bit of the cutting mat. Utilize wide, even strokes that go right over the mat. Do whatever it takes not to get any paste on the edges of the mat. On the off chance that you do, simply clear it off right away.

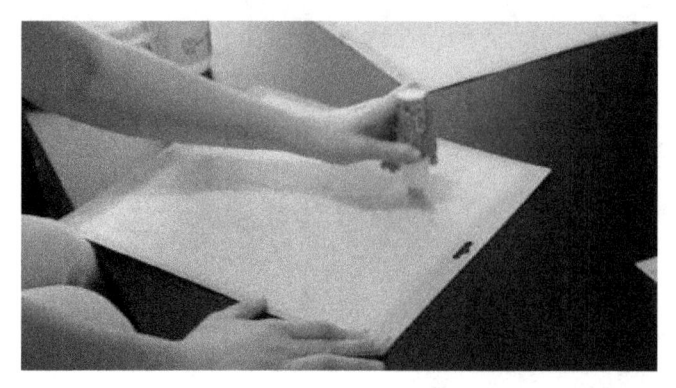

2. Permit the mat to dry for 20 to 30 minutes. The paste should turn clear.

3. In the event that your mat appears to be unreasonably clingy for cutting fragile materials, you can utilize a spotless shirt or bit of texture to condition it. More than once press the texture against every single clingy territory of your cutting mat. This will pull off a portion of the overabundance glue, and coat your mat with a touch of build up to mitigate it an indent.

4. Hold up a couple of hours before covering recently stuck mats with the reasonable film spread, so it doesn't stall out to the outside of your mat.

Cautioning: *Do not get any paste on the edges of the cutting mat, as this can get onto the rollers of your Cricut or Silhouette, and jam your machine.*

The Different ways

You can utilize other shower cements or shabby pastes appropriate for mats. Since these techniques are route messier than the paste pen, you should cover the edges of the mat with veiling tape to shield them from the paste.

Best decision for splash glue:

- Krylon Easy Tack Repositionable Adhesive Spray

Best decision for tasteless paste:

- Aleene's Tack it Over and Over

Tips for Taking Care of Your Cutting Mats

If you take great consideration of your cutting mats, they'll take great consideration of you, and your wallet. Here are some broad consideration tips for your Cricut cutting mats: Cover your mats when not being used.

Keep the unmistakable film spread that accompanied your cutting mat, and supplant the spread when you are finished utilizing it. This will forestall residue, hairs, and filaments from amassing on the clingy surface of the mat. It might assist with taking a sharpie and imprint "TOP" on the top side of the unmistakable acetic acid derivation spread, so it's anything but difficult to supplant accurately.

Try not to manhandle abuse your mats.

Dodge too much contacting the clingy surface of the mat with your hands, as this can erode and harm the cement after some time. (This is particularly valid for Cricut's pink texture mats!) Use the best possible apparatuses: spatulas, tweezers, and scrubbers to expel cuts and scraps from your cutting mat. This will secure your mats, just as keep your completed cut tasks from twisting and tearing. At the point when you do need to contact your mats, utilize perfect, dry hands that are liberated from salve.

Constantly clean your mat.

Start utilizing a clingy build up roller and infant wipes to clean the outside of your cutting mats. This will keep them perfect and crisp for each undertaking.

Tips for Drying Cutting Mats

- Let your mat evaporate totally by hanging it, or essentially setting it upstanding in your dish rack. After you've washed it, you need to ensure the two sides can get dry, so don't simply leave it sitting on your counter.

- Try not to utilize heat, as warmth may make your cutting mat split or twist, making it never again fit in your cutting machine. This implies no hair dryers!
- If you have to accelerate the drying time, you can point a fan at your mat to build air flow. I guess utilizing a hair dryer on the "Cool" setting ought to be fine, as long as you can believe yourself to not go through any warmth to speed the procedure. No utilization crushing your last mat just to find a new line of work completed quicker! (Despite the fact that I figure you ought to consistently have a couple additional mats around.)

Chapter Four

What materials would I be able to cut with my Cricut?

Something lovely about The Cricut machine is all the various materials you can cut with it. At the point when I originally was acquainted with the Cricut machine years prior, I thought it was something utilized uniquely to cut paper. My companion made huge amounts of adorable natively constructed cards, and I cherished making those with her, yet I didn't figure I could ever need my own Cricut in light of the fact that I don't make a huge amount of paper makes. A year ago I got the opportunity to converse with her from Cricut at a New Year's eve occasion and she clarified all the stuff you can make utilizing the Cricut machine. That night we made some adorable paper pendant flags as a venture.

Be that as it may, she additionally cut out the gathering's photograph setting out of some light cardboard material and even cut out some vinyl for the area we were at in light of the fact that their store hours had fallen off the window. I was intrigued.

Since I have had my machine I have utilized it to cut felt for a pennant, card stock, paper, vinyl, sparkle vinyl, sparkle iron-on, standard iron-on, and false calfskin just to give some examples materials. It likewise has the ability to cut chipboard.

Cricut Explore and Cricut Maker machines cut such a significant number of materials that as far as possible is your creative mind. From something as sensitive as tissue paper to thick cowhide, these stunning machines can do everything.

Significant: *Cricut Explore and Maker machines are not nourishment safe, and can't cut fondant or comparative materials.*

What materials would you be able to use with your Cricut machine? You'll be flabbergasted at this rundown of 100+ various materials a Cricut machine can cut!

Numerous individuals think a Cricut machine is only for cutting paper or vinyl, yet it can accomplish such a great deal more than that! There are more than 100 unique materials that a Cricut Explore machine can cut, and the new Cricut Maker has a rotating blade and a profound blade sharp edge that can cut considerably more!

So in case you're considering what various materials a Cricut machine can cut, look at this magnificent rundown underneath!

The Ultimate List of Over 100 Materials a Cricut Machine Can Cut

A Cricut Explore machine can cut practically anything as long as it is 2.0mm thick or more slender. What's more, on the off chance that you have a Cricut Maker, that machine has 10x the cutting power and can slice materials up to 2.4mm thick!

Cardstock and Paper

The Cricut is extraordinary at cutting paper and cardstock, yet it doesn't simply cut scrapbook paper! Look at all the various types of paper a Cricut machine can cut:

- Adhesive Cardstock
- Cardstock
- Grain Box
- Development Paper
- Duplicate Paper
- Level Cardboard
- Run Cardstock
- Run Paper
- Foil Embossed Paper
- Foil Poster Board
- Cooler Paper

- Sparkle Cardstock
- Sparkle Paper
- Kraft Board
- Kraft Paper
- Metallic Cardstock
- Metallic Paper
- Metallic Poster Board
- Journal Paper
- Paper Grocery Bags
- Material Paper
- Paper Board
- Pearl Cardstock
- Pearl Paper
- Photos
- Photograph Framing Mat
- Post Its
- Blurb Board
- Rice Paper
- Scrapbook Paper
- Sparkle Paper
- Strong Core Cardstock
- Watercolor Paper
- Wax Paper
- White Core Cardstock

Vinyl

Another incredible material that the Cricut machine can cut is vinyl. Vinyl is amazing for making signs, decals, stencils, designs, and so forth.

- Adhesive Vinyl
- Blackboard Vinyl
- Dry Erase Vinyl
- Sparkle Vinyl
- Shiny Vinyl
- Holographic Vinyl
- Matte Vinyl
- Metallic Vinyl
- Outside Vinyl
- Printable Vinyl
- Stencil Vinyl

Iron On

Iron on vinyl, otherwise called warmth move vinyl, is one of my preferred materials to cut with my Cricut! You can utilize iron on vinyl to finish shirts, tote sacks, or some other texture thing.

- Rushed Iron On
- Foil Iron On
- Sparkle Iron On
- Lustrous Iron On
- Holographic Sparkle Iron On

- Matte Iron On
- Metallic Iron On
- Neon Iron On
- Printable Iron On

<u>Textures and Textiles</u>

The Cricut works superbly at cutting textures, however you unquestionably need to include a stabilizer like Wonder Under or Heat'n Bond before cutting. These textures and materials can be cut with a Cricut Explore machine, yet there are much more that you can cut with the rotational blade on a Cricut Maker machine.

- Burlap
- Canvas
- Cotton Fabric
- Denim
- Duck Cloth
- False Leather
- False Suede
- Felt
- Wool
- Calfskin
- Cloth
- Metallic Leather
- Oil Cloth
- Polyester

- Printable Fabric
- Silk
- Fleece Felt

Different Materials

Other than texture, paper, and vinyl, there are huge amounts of other claim to fame materials a Cricut can cut too. Here are a lot of fun thoughts!

- Adhesive Foil
- Adhesive Wood
- Aluminum Sheets
- Aluminum Foil
- Balsa Wood
- Birch Wood
- Stopper Board
- Layered Paper
- Specialty Foam
- Pipe Tape
- Embossable Foil
- Foil Acetate
- Sparkle Foam
- Magnet Sheets
- Metallic Vellum
- Paint Chips
- Plastic Packaging

- Printable Magnet Sheets
- Printable Sticker Paper
- Psychologist Plastic
- Soft drink Can
- Stencil Material
- Tissue Paper
- Transitory Tattoo Paper
- Straightforwardness Film
- Vellum
- Washi Sheets
- Washi Tape
- Window Cling
- Wood Veneer
- Wrapping Paper

Cricut Maker

In the event that you have the Maker, you can cut considerably more things! The Cricut Maker has 10x the cutting power of the Explore machines; in addition, it has a rotational sharp edge and a blade edge that enable it to cut significantly more materials. The Cricut Maker can slice materials up to 2.4mm thick, in addition to over 125+ kinds of texture, including:

- Chiffon
- Cashmere
- Fleece

- Jersey
- Jute
- Knits
- Moleskin
- Muslin
- Seersucker
- Terry Cloth
- Tulle
- Tweed
- Velvet

What Kind Of simple Crafts and Projects Can I Make with My Cricut Machine?

In case you're searching for an enjoyment summer venture or another DIY planter idea at that point look no further. This task is too straightforward.

1. Sewing Star Pallet Sign

Where to get recovered wood, Amazon truly sells everything.

Amazon currently sells bed wood signs, so not any more attempting to rescue wood and amass it just to follow a pattern.

Bed wood signs can be bought in two distinct sizes by the most current hot Amazon dealer called 48×40. The bed signs come in two unique sizes, little and huge. The bigger size is being utilized for this task.

Okay, expecting you have acquired your bed sign and Amazon has incredibly sent it to you in two days, this is what else you need; scrapbook paper in the shades of your decision, Mod Podge, a paper trimmer, and a paint brush. On the off chance that you are one of my Cricut peeps, you can feel free to cut your paper with the Design Space document.

To begin, you need to initially cut squares at 4.5"x4.5" inches. You should resize these relying upon your bed sign measurements. I would propose slicing a couple to begin and ensuring they don't feel too huge or little for your sign. Next, cut your squares down the middle to make the triangles. You will require sixteen triangles for one sign.

Utilizing your Mod Podge, coat the wood sheets and the rear of your triangles. Spot the triangles each in turn on the board, covering the top with another meager layer of Mod Podge. Permit your sign to totally dry, and afterward give it a last layer of Mod Podge. I really made two of these signs and utilized both a matte and lustrous Mod Podge finish, and both worked extraordinary. I lean toward the vibe of the reflexive, however don't hesitate to pick whatever you like.

That is it! So natural. Last tip, in the event that you are searching for bed sign thoughts, 48×40 has huge amounts of them on its site. Absolutely worth looking at!

Supports to 48×40 making an item that incredibly diminishes my need to work with corroded nails and end up with a lockjaw shot.

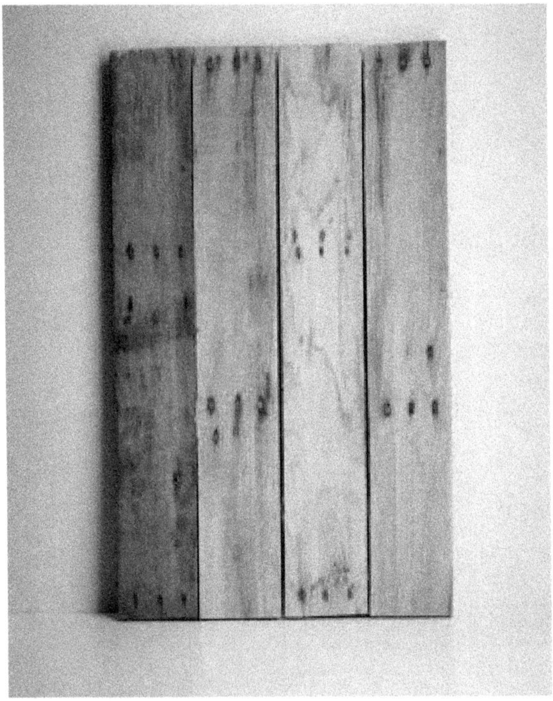

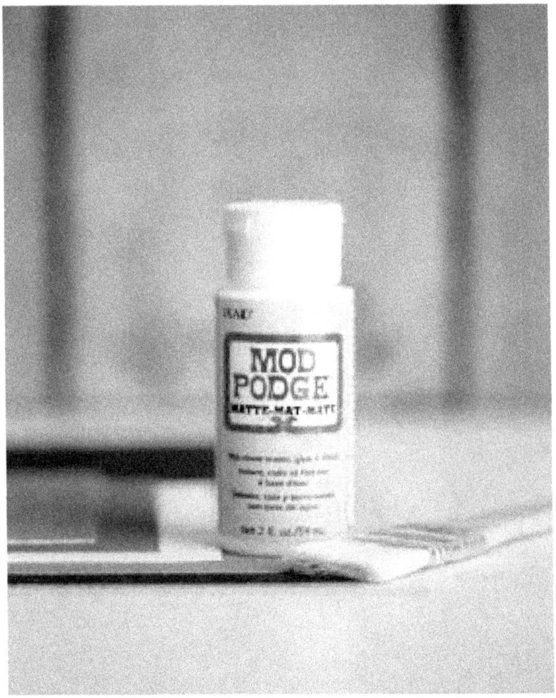
MOD
PODGE
MATTE-MAT-MATE

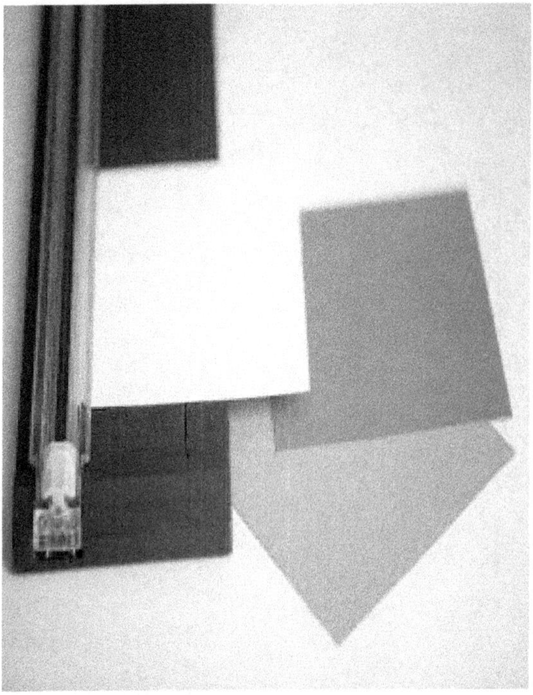

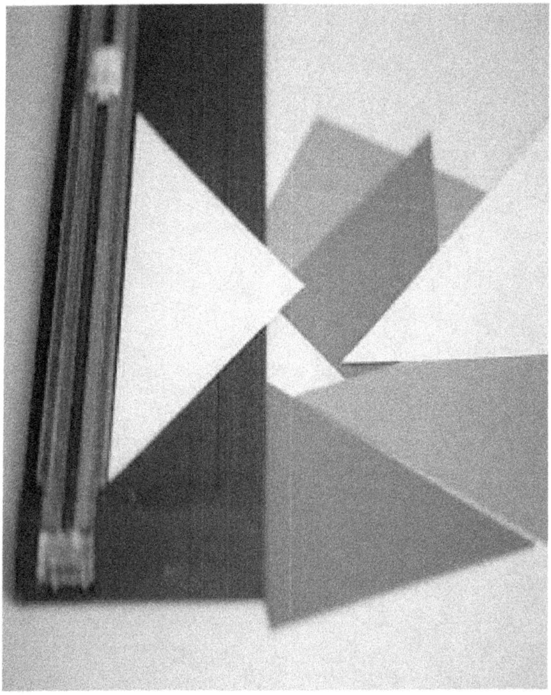

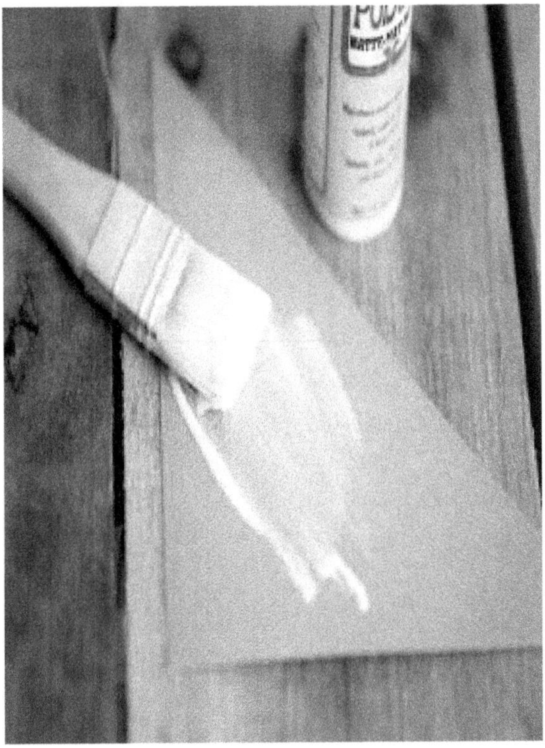

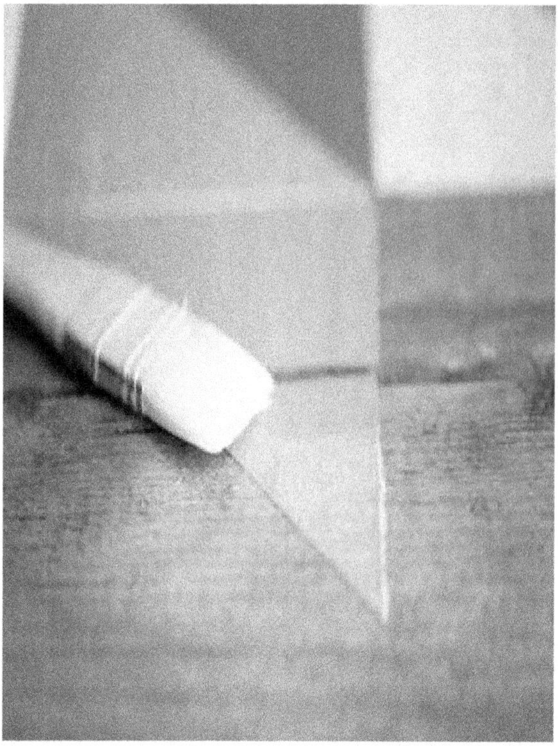

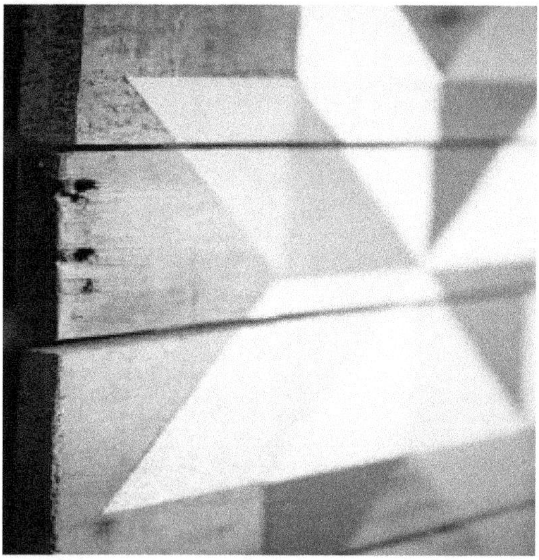

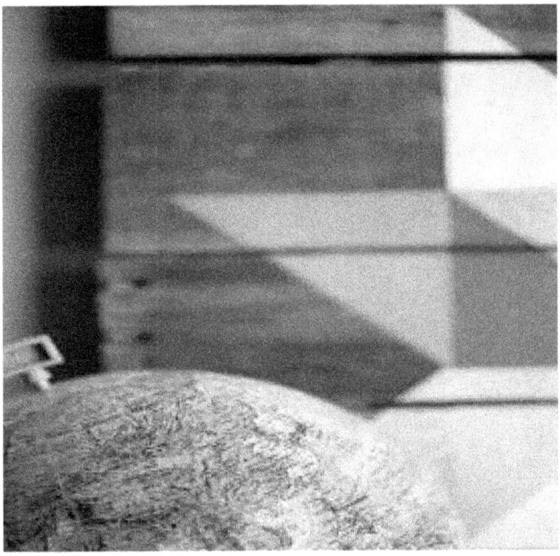

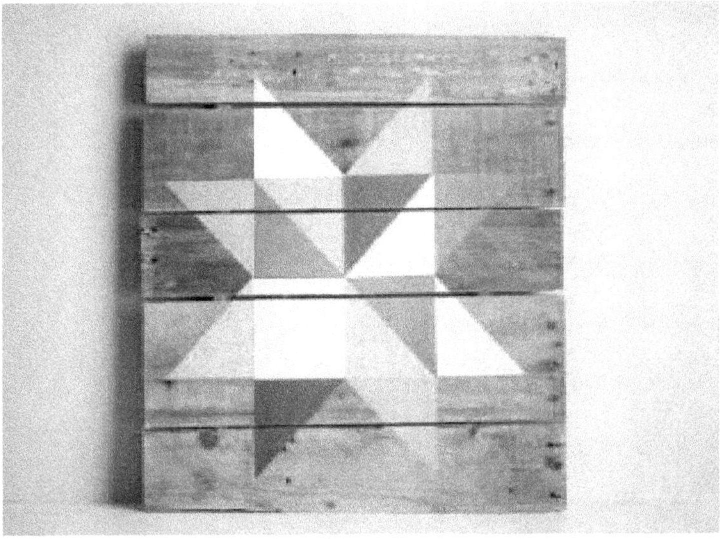

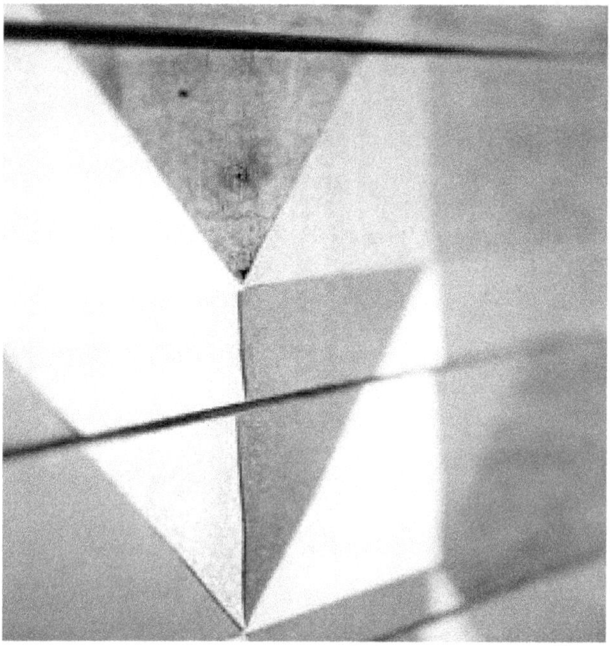

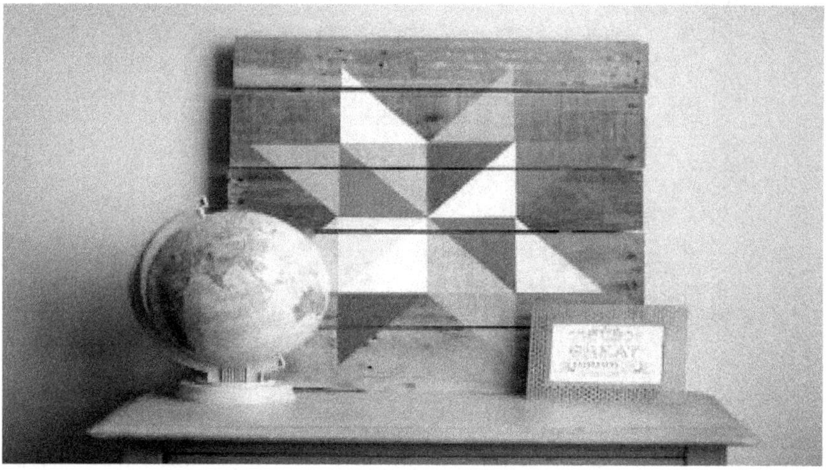

2. DIAMOND HANGING PLANTERS

Diamond Hanging Planters Creating custom style has consistently been one of my interests, regardless of whether it's making something without any preparation or making an old thing new again there is something fulfilling about it. Like I've referenced before I love to change my stylistic layout regularly which can be an exorbitant propensity. Some of the time I discover something I simply begin to look all starry eyed at and must have. It might fall in my financial limit, typically in the event that it doesn't I attempt to discover an approach to DIY my own variant. The Diamond Hanging Planters I'm sharing today are actually that sort of task!

Supplies:

- Cricut Explore Air
- Standard Grip or Strong Grip Cutting Mat
- Profound Cut Blade
- Chipboard, 50pt
- Paste firearm or fast dry paste
- DecoArt acrylic paint, ocean glass and dim sky
- Froth brushes
- Calfskin cording
- Light covering tape
- Wire, discretionary
- Succulents, live or fake

- Little plastic compartment of soil if utilizing live succulents
- Little white rock, mine is fish tank rock

I made a few pictures in Photoshop for the jewel structure and transferred them to Design Space. The base triangle boards estimated 2.3 wide x 2.82". The top trapezoid boards estimated 2.3 wide x 0.76". You will just need 6 boards of each, however it's in every case best to cut at any rate 2 extra simply incase.

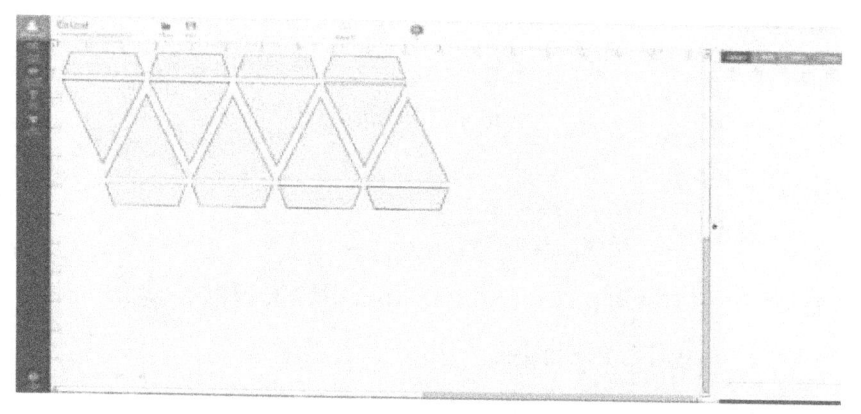

You will choose the custom setting on the cutting dial. At that point select Chipboard Heavy, 0.7mm – and hit GO. When the principal cut is finished, hit GO again and send it through for a subsequent time.

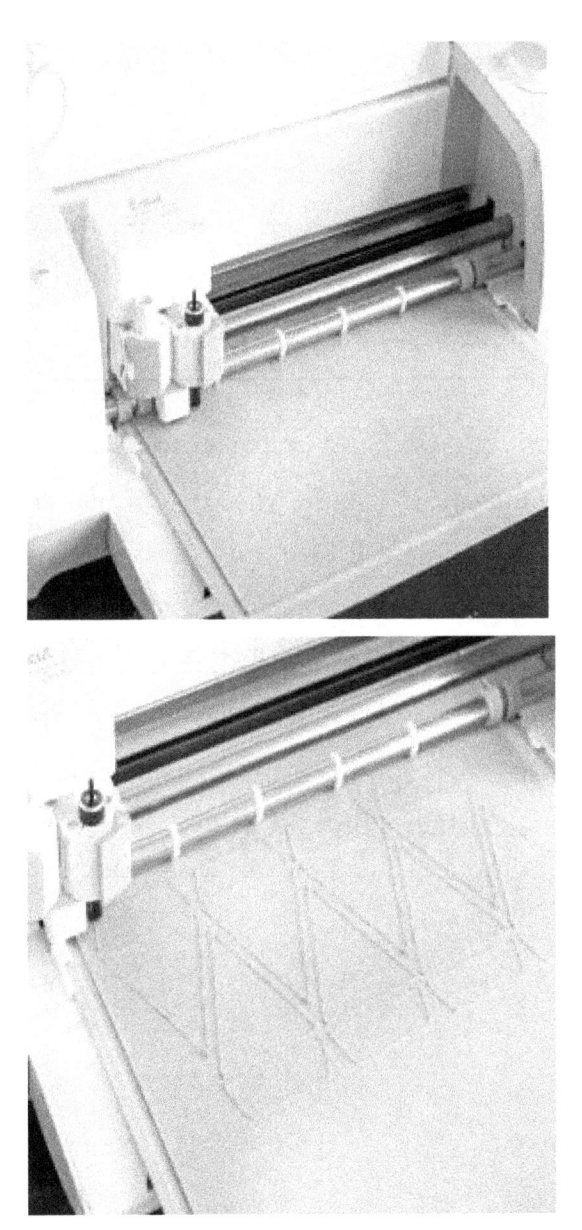

When every one of the boards are sliced you should amass them for sticking. I arranged each of the 6 triangle boards as close as could be allowed, holding them set up as I utilized a light concealing tape to hold them together.

Presently include your trapezoid pieces a similar route to the top like demonstrated as follows.

Close your jewel shape with another bit of light veiling tape. Additionally, delicately tape all the trapezoid sorts out as well so the whole jewel shape is finished before sticking.

With either a paste weapon or fast dry paste you should stick the outside creases of the jewel. All the taped pieces ought to be within. In the event that utilizing a paste weapon be cautioned it's going be dubious in case you're not use to working speedy with craft glue. I utilized craft glue for mine and when I spread the line of paste down the crease I utilized my finger to smooth away any overabundance stick so it didn't leave an uneven surface. In the event that you need to spare your fingers you can utilize the snappy dry paste, make certain to tidy up any overabundance stick. Allow everything to dry. When it's dry expel all the tape from within.

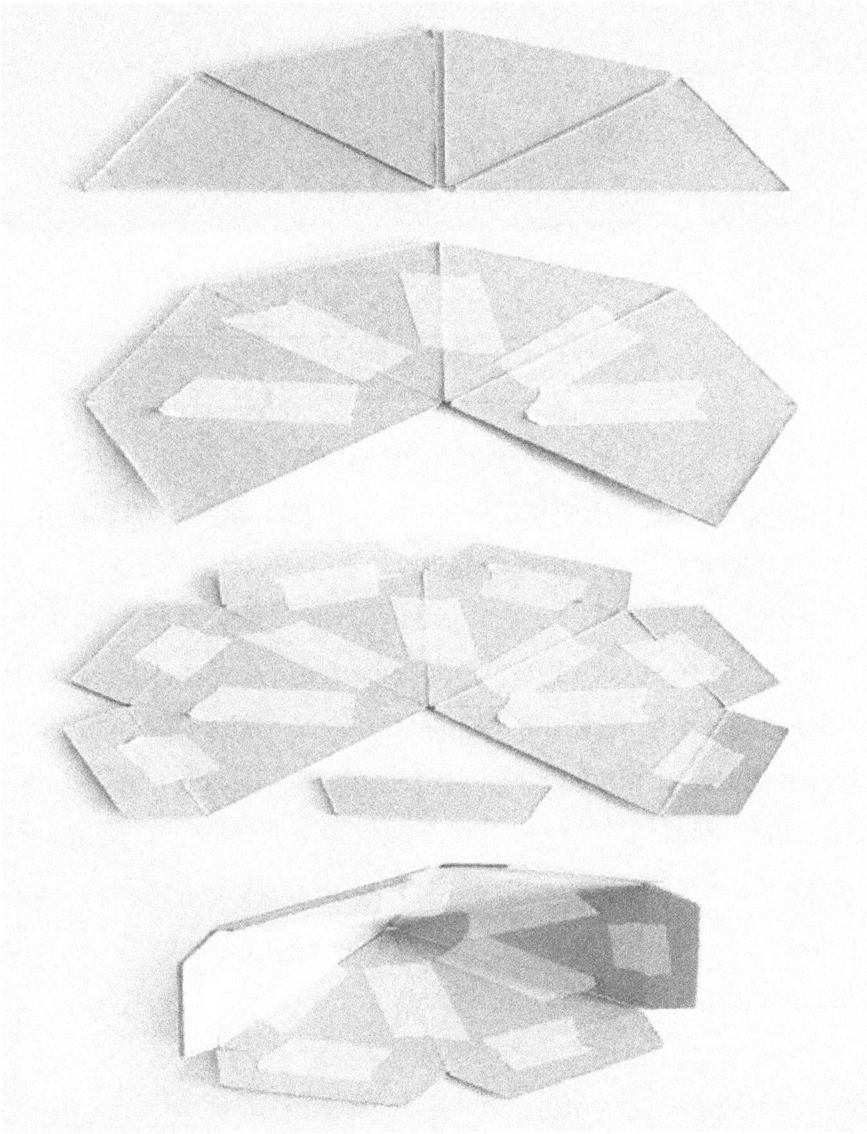

Since you're left with this amazing precious stone shape you should make the gaps for the cowhide cording to hang them. I utilized a customary opening punch.

I kept my hues unpretentious when it came to painting. I needed them to be delicate like the succulents that would go inside them. I utilized my preferred BB Frosch Chalk Paint Powder blended in with my most loved DecoArt paints to make paint with incredible inclusion. It's ideal for covering paste and you will possibly require two light layers of paint in the event that you utilize the chalk paint powder.

At the point when your paint is dry it's an ideal opportunity to include the cowhide cording. You can either craft glue it to within the precious stone grower or tie a bunch at last that goes within the grower.

I included some gold wire I had close by to combine the two strands at the top for hanging. This is discretionary, yet added some extra to them.

Since these Diamond Hanging Planters are made out of chipboard clearly they aren't waterproof like my motivation for this task. You can either put fake succulents inside with little white rock (I discovered mine at the pet store, it's fish rock) or you can put a little plastic compartment loaded up with soil inside with the live succulents, at that point spread with the little white rock to conceal the holder. In the event that you do the live form you will simply need to water it cautiously.

I set live succulents in mine since I have a wealth at this moment; it is by all accounts the main plants I can't slaughter. In the long run I may change them out to counterfeit if the watering becomes too hard.

These would likewise make adorable little coordinators on a work area or bookshelf, wouldn't you say? Simply skirt the gap punch and calfskin cording and viola!

The best piece of this task, other than these being such a lot of fun? They cost about $3 to make since I had the paint, wire, succulents close by.

I love that the Cricut Explore Air has totally changed my way to deal with creating and DIY! It's made it such a great amount of simpler to make ventures like these enjoyment Diamond Hanging Planters, loads of custom exceptional stylistic theme, and snappy tasks on the fly. It's such a great amount of enjoyable to consider some fresh possibilities while making these undertakings, and I love that I'm not cutting a huge amount of pieces by hand and that I can make remotely anyplace. It's actually my most loved specialty apparatus, without a doubt! How might the Cricut Explore Air change your way to deal with DIY and Crafting? Leave a remark I'd love to hear!